D0469046

Kicking Ass on the Road

The Ultimate Guide for the Solo Woman Traveler

Sunni Dawson

This book is a work of nonfiction based on the life, experiences, and recollections of the author. Some of the names of people or places, dates, sequences, or the detail of events have been changed.

Cover design by Miladinka Milic (www.milagraphicartist.com).

Disclaimer

All material in this book is provided for your information only and may not be construed as advice or instruction. No action or inaction should be taken based solely on the contents of this information; instead, readers should consult the appropriate professionals on any matter relating to their health, insurance, travel and well-being.

The information and opinions expressed here are believed to be accurate, based on the best judgment available to the author, and readers who fail to consult with the appropriate authorities assume the risk of any injuries. The author and publishers are not responsible for errors or omissions.

About the Author

Sunni Dawson is a writer, coach and speaker. She has traveled and lived all over the world for the best part of 5 years. She is passionate about living brave, helping people step outside their comfort zones, curious about what makes people change and loves connecting with people from around the globe. She adores solo travel, cooking and photography. Some of her previous work incarnations include: lawyer, strategic and business planner, call centre chick, diversity specialist, law lecturer and a vego cook for a child care centre.

Check out Sunni's work:

www.sunnidawson.com

YouTube: Sunni Dawson

Facebook: www.facebook.com/sunnidawson

Twitter: www.twitter.com/sunnidawson

Instagram: @sunnidawson

Join the Live Brave FB Community! People who are living brave, making changes, taking risks and supporting each other along the way. Come and be a part of it.

https://web.facebook.com/groups/livebrave/

or email us: livebrave@groups.facebook.com

"You'll never find out unless you go."

Sunni Dawson

Table of Contents

1. So you're thinking of going solo?

"You are traveling alone?" He looked at me with a heady mix of horror, pity and curiosity.

I gave him a broad smile. I was well and truly practiced at this by now.

"Estoy feliz… I'm happy."

He smiled back, somewhat incredulous, "Are you married?"

This was code for: you should be married and at home leading a decent life with a family. Not on your own enjoying yourself, especially at your age. But if you are alone and enjoying yourself, I want in on that.

"No. Estoy feliz," I repeated affirmatively, shaking my head for emphasis.

"How long you here for?"

"Another couple of days."

"What are you doing tonight?" *What a surprise!*

"I'm tired, I'm going back to sleep early in my hotel."

This was a standard conversation I had all over South and Central America, parts of Europe and Asia.

Both women and men found it surprising that I traveled by myself. Alone. I figured the best way to approach it was to exude confidence and happiness. I got hassled less that way. But the truth is, I was happy.

Really happy.

Travel is rich with emotions, great highs, some lows, inward and outward growth, challenges big and small, inspiration and life. Solo travel is all of this, doubled. I love putting myself into incredibly different places and spaces and absorbing all it has to offer. From tropical beaches where the king of reggae reigns, to solo sunrises over ancient temples, to wandering 11th Century cobblestoned streets, I love knowing that I can travel to most places by myself, or with others, with relative ease. It takes both practice and technique to be comfortable and confident almost anywhere.

A little about me. I was a late bloomer. I didn't start traveling until my early 30s. This was for a variety of reasons such as my focus on developing my career and not wanting to go for long periods of time away from my friends and family. I also had a partner for about 4 1/2 years who didn't want to travel. So I didn't.

However, I've made up for it. Through a variety of fortuitous circumstances (and taking loads of risks - more on this later), I have traveled and lived abroad for the best part of the last 5 years or so. I want to share with you some of what I've learnt along the way. My aim is to make your steps, leaps or bounds into travel smooth, easy and fun.

This book will help all women travelers and anyone who is thinking about taking the plunge into solo travel. It will help you plan, research and craft your short or longer journeys. There are many varied approaches that solo women travelers have employed to have fantastic abroad experiences. I want to share with you strategies that I've learnt, tested out and refined over the last 5 years. I know that these tools and techniques will give you a fabulous start to your amazing adventures.

Some of the reasons you could be reading this book:

- You'd like to investigate traveling solo. This book will get you there!
- You are the ultimate preparer. Great. This book will give you everything you need to prepare for your adventure.
- You're looking for ways to travel cheaply. There are loads of tips for this throughout this book and particularly in the final chapter.
- You'd like to feel more independent. This book will help you become an independent and confident traveler.
- You want some inspirations for your own travels and long vacations or gap years. There are loads of options and tips I've detailed on this (particularly in the final chapter).

- You don't have much time to prepare. You've got everything you need to do right here.

- You're ready to push your limits, learn more about yourself and step out on your own, and you'd like strategies on how to do that. This book has you covered.

- You have traveled by yourself and you'd like to read some stories you're familiar with or get tips for your new adventures. You'll find all that inside this book.

- You like a good travel story. You'll get a few of those!

Please know that you are never too old, too fat, too pretty, too ugly, too tired or whatever the dominating voice in the back of your head is saying, to start traveling or do any of what I talk about in this book. I really want to encourage you and this book shows you, in detail, how you can take those first steps. I want to hear about your stories when you do!

How this guide can help you:

- It will give you everything you need to prepare for the adventure of a lifetime (or two:))!

- If you are considering traveling solo, but feeling nervous or overwhelmed.

- You think that solo travel will be boring because it's just traveling with you. Believe me, it never ends up just being with you (you are guaranteed to meet people along the way and the best part is, it's your choice if you want to spend time with them or not). It could also be a great antidote for you. Having time to spend by yourself is one of the most valuable life learnings you can have.

- Stretch yourself beyond your comfort zone through practical, time tested techniques.

- It will help you understand, prepare for and feel that you can be a strong, safe and independent traveler.

- Prepare you to have enormous amounts of fun and share some amazing experiences with new friends.

- If you think that solo travel is absolutely not for you, that's okay. You'll enjoy reading the stories and advice anyway. And just maybe, just maybe…

How to use this guide

I have set out this guide in easy to follow chapters to help you prepare and plan for your travels, as well as my tips on how to enjoy your time as much as possible when you're there. The book is written so that you can flick to the chapter you need at any particular time. I've also included handy checklists and mind maps that you can use at any stage prior or during your journey. I do recommend reading the guide in its entirety before you leave, as there are lessons, tips and strategies throughout. If you know about them in advance, you will be prepared for almost anything.

The rewards of solo travel

To begin this book on the right note, I'd like to introduce you to the rewards of solo travel. There are just so many! Of course there are detractions, and we will work through those in the coming chapters, but to begin with, I want to give you the gems.

You feel stronger in you

I remember walking along the beach in the Gili Islands after a week of ups and downs in mainland Bali. I had been cheated out of a lot of money by a taxi driver, a tour guide, a massage lady and my hotel. I also had some beautiful walks, succulent food and seen monkeys for the first time. But having made my way to these beautiful islands with no motorized transport, white sand and warm luminous waters, I felt somewhat at peace with it.

I did it by myself. It was challenging. I saw some gorgeous sights along the way. I felt that if I could come through what I had gone through in the past week, I could do more things by myself. And enjoy them. I felt it was possible.

The good and bad aspects of travel allow you to feel stronger in what you can do by yourself. It makes you understand that a lot more is possible for you.

You feel free

There is nothing like that feeling after checking in and sitting in the waiting lounge before your flight, or as the plane lifts off, or walking out into a different world full of strange new things. It's that jittery excitement, the wide eyed awe, anticipation of the good things that await. Cocktails, music, staying up late, sleeping in, complete dominion over what you choose to do, whenever you want to do it, is what it's all about. You have a greater choice. You don't have to give into your boss's impositions, you don't have the everyday family demands, or obligations of same old routines. Most importantly, you don't have to do what your traveling companion wants or needs to do. You have complete freedom and choice over what you do. And it is just so sweet!

You meet amazing people & see amazing things

I've met some of the most interesting and thoughtful people on my journeys around the world. I've been lucky to get to know them on a deeper level and I think a lot of this has to do with traveling solo. I'm more available to spend hours / days with new friends. I love this. Having the time to connect closely with people that inspire you is just perfect in my mind.

Another aspect to solo travel is seeing the things I enjoy the most. I determine what I want to see and when. I love art galleries and I know not everyone does. Also, I'm a mad hobby photographer and I adore being able to spend inordinate amounts of time at a beautiful spot to get just the right picture. When I'm with others, I'm conscious of this and I rush. This for me is a huge benefit of going solo.

You can survive

If you've ever traveled on a train in India (even in first class) and survived the toileting experience, then you know that you can survive anything. Seriously. All and everything. Anything.

Trains in India (and also in most other southeast Asian countries), are a bit special. If they have first class, it usually resembles what we would consider 'very basic travel' or let's just say sixth class. There are no 'first class' toilets either. The toilets are the same throughout the train and are used by everyone and anyone. There is no escape.

Entering a standard train toilet in these countries, you are always greeted by multiple coats of grime, furry green animals growing out of corners, never ever any toilet paper and rarely a sink that has a functional running tap. The worst is the slimy, slippery, dry-heave inducing hole that you are obliged to squat over (and, dear women, if you are having the unfortunate timing of your menstruation, quite simply, it is hell).

You then realize you can survive, and that you are more resilient than you ever thought.

You can learn about you and others to a deeper level

I literally have had hundreds of experiences where I've been sitting in a cafe or restaurant and somehow a conversation has started with a person or couple of people on the next table. After the usual, 'How long have you been here?' and the gold 'How long are you traveling for?' (which equates in some people's book as 'How big are your genitals?') the chat often turns to life.

How happy and free most people are in the moment (I would say that 90% of people I've met traveling, and this is adding up to a substantial number of people now, feel this way), and how they are dreading going home. Often the discussions turn to deeper subjects such as religion, cultural practices and expanding understandings of why we do what we do.

I regularly walk away thoroughly enriched by these exchanges. I have had a chance to reflect on my own life, what I do, and regularly the world at large through discussions with fellow travelers.

Knowing you can do anything and go anywhere

After coming back from that first vacation, or even during the vacation, you begin to realize something. You've done it. You've taken the first step. You've found your way in new lands. You've learnt and seen new things. You've relaxed. You've partied. You've tasted. You've done it for yourself.

And you know what? Once you've done it once, you can do it again. And the joy is even sweeter and more delightful, knowing that perhaps you can expand your reach, or come back and enjoy more fully the places you've been before.

You can do it. You can do anything and go anywhere. How great is that?

Traveling isn't always easy but it's such a fun adventure

I love travel, and I believe it just gets better. Travel certainly is challenging. You are nearly always out of your comfort zone. It's tiring and sometimes you are pushed to the point of seemingly never ending tears, but it's also inspiring, eye opening, gratifying and liberating.

It's an adventure. And aren't adventures fun?

This guide is designed to help you get the most out of your travel experiences. I've covered in detail the suck-full moments that you may experience so that you can be prepared. When you're prepared, you can relax, knowing you've got it covered. Most importantly, this book is about enabling you to have the most fun and fulfilling time you can whilst you're away.

So join me in planning your ultimate adventure.

2. Preparation, preparation, preparation!

The biggest thing I learnt from law school was: Preparation, Preparation, Preparation! Those that win are the ones that are the most prepared. Fail to prepare and you kiss your case goodbye (I wish we were all like those fabulously smart TV show lawyers that get all the key materials immediately and come out with the cleverest lines in an instant).

I have written this book with this in mind. I want you to have a fantastic holiday/break/rambling travel across the globe. This book will definitely help get you there.

First tip: Get clear!

One thing to do before you set out on this marvelous path of adventure is to work out your purpose for traveling. Do you want to relax? Do you want to see new things? Do you want to eat new foods? (I have one friend who proudly says the only reason she travels is to eat. Go girl!).

There are so many reasons why you may want to travel and it may be a combination of things. Why do I think it's important to get clear on why you are traveling? Because it can give you a focus. If for example, you want to have a complete break, you may plan on more relaxing activities and more beach time than exploration. If you want to explore culture, you may want to organize your travels around seeing and experiencing as much of this as possible.

You may want to learn a new skill (painting, sky diving, language) or to volunteer. Your plans can center around this.

Think about what you want to achieve at the end:

- A feeling of relaxation?
- Seeing a particular sight you've always wanted to visit?
- Finding out that you can cope with time by yourself?
- Doing something that scares you?
- Time for reflection and self-discovery?
- Finish a book?
- Learn a new skill?
- Finding adventure and new experiences?
- Practice a hobby you love?
- Experiencing different cultures and ways of living?

By asking yourself these questions before you go, you can prepare for the travel experience that focuses on your goals. Also, during your travels, you can go back to these questions and ask yourself whether you are meeting your objective. If you're not, you might be ok with that (and have discovered something more pleasurable) or you could refocus your time so that you are meeting your goal/goals.

There are so many paths or options for any aim you may have. For example, you may want to try meditation. Literally, thousands of places teach meditation around the world. The varieties of meditation courses to choose from is just the beginning. Do you want to do the course by the beach or in the mountains? Do you want to stay close to home? Do you want to travel further afield post the course and/or combine a visit to see friends? The options for just about everything are endless.

Group tours & the type of travel

After deciding on your key goal/goals for this trip, it is then worth determining the sort of travel you want to do at this time. Do you want to join tours and be met at airports, or do you want to book things yourself? Do you want to go to touristy areas or do you want to get off the beaten track? This will help you define how much research and preparation you will need to do before you go.

If you decide to join a group tour, the level of in-country preparation will be a lot less. The tour company at minimum will book your accommodation and travel between places. Some group tours organize everything for you: meals, transfers and activities. Other group tours offer more independence, booking accommodation and travel only, allowing you to do the activities you want to do during the day. You choose whether you want to join the group members for dinners and/or other activities.

If you are a first time traveler, a group tour can be a good start to get familiar with traveling. It's also generally a lot safer. If you are more independent, go for a tour that allows you the flexibility to explore what interests you in a particular location. If you'd like to just sit back and take it all in, go for a more planned tour.

When you start to research group tours, you will see a great variety of companies and style of travel. Some cater for the very young or mature age group, but there are many that have a real mix of ages. Once I was in a travel group with some 18 year olds, a 29 year old, a 38 year old, a 57 year old and a 68 year old and we all got along very well.

Another option is to do a tour for part of your holiday. You could do some of your own travel and some with a tour group. Another benefit of joining a tour group is that you get to meet and share experiences for extended lengths of time with other travelers. You can and do meet other travelers outside of a tour group, but it's guaranteed in a tour. A detraction is if you don't get along with other members of your group. If you are on your own, this is quick and easy to fix!

It all comes down to what you want to feel like at the end of the holiday. Do you want a stronger sense of independence? Do you want to just have things done for you, so you can sit back and enjoy the ride? Do you want a combination of organized and free flowing?

Checklist for determining your goals

- ✔ What are your goal/goals at this time?

- ✔ Is there a particular place(s) you need to do this in?

- ✔ If there is no particular place, are you feeling like more beach, mountain, desert or plains time?

- ✔ Is there a country or countries you would prefer to be in?

- ✔ What are the cost differences between each country and/or course?

- ✔ Do you need to develop any skills to go to this country or place (i.e. learning a language or being more physically fit?)

- ✔ Do you want to book and do everything yourself or do you want have someone else help with the organization and travel (such as joining a tour and/or getting an agent to book it all for you)?

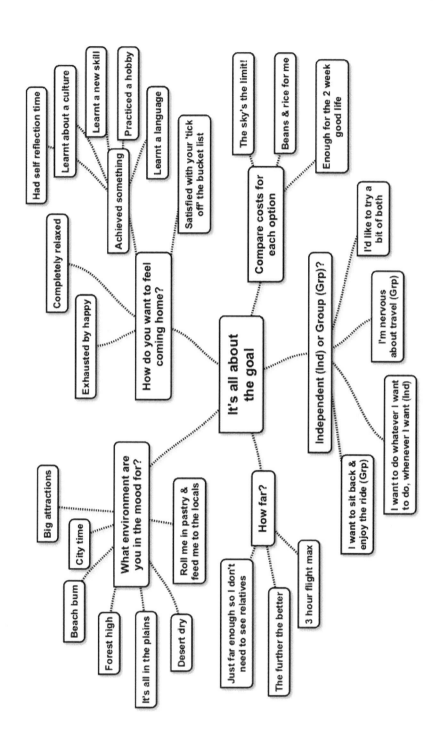

Research & planning

Traveling overseas requires an extensive amount of preparation. The rest of this chapter details all the fundamental things you will need to consider, plan and research for your trip. This chapter covers the essentials for any travel. If you want to specifically focus your plans on cheap travel and/or living abroad for a length of time, also read the final chapter 'Traveling and living on the cheap'.

Visas

Visa requirements vary throughout the world depending on where you are from and where you are going to. Some countries update and change their visa requirements regularly, so check with the country's embassy before you go. Depending on how long you are intending on staying, you may need to exit and re-enter the country during your stay to continue the currency of the visa.

Travel insurance

I have been shocked recently to meet a few travelers traveling without travel insurance. I don't know whether it's because I'm anal or a lawyer but the financial and other implications like stress (trying to organize things in a foreign place when you're stressed, sick and potentially alone) seems nonsensical to me.

Depending on the country you end up in, a broken ankle could cost you upwards of $5000 after x-rays and doctors' fees. Then there is ongoing treatment. This in itself seems enough reason to pay a few hundred dollars for travel insurance before you depart (note there are a couple of travel insurance companies that allow you to take out travel insurance if you're already abroad, but you have a lot more options before you leave & it also means if you have problems with your initial flights, you are covered).

Be very careful with credit card travel insurance!

Most importantly, be careful of credit card travel insurance. Really. Get onto the credit card insurance website, review the terms and download the product disclosure statement. There are just so many limits to credit card insurance, and you really should be aware about whether it fulfills your current and future traveling needs.

Review the below list before you decide whether to rely solely on your credit card travel insurance.

Things to review with your prospective travel insurance company:

- Review the comprehensive versus basic terms. Basic is usually very basic. If you are only carrying a small bag full of clothes, then just covering emergency hospitalization may be fine. However, if you are carrying an expensive camera, you may want to reconsider this.
- Cameras, computer and music equipment etc. Most policies have a limit for each item. Check how expensive each of your items are and whether the particular type of insurance covers it.

- Most policies don't cover you having an alcoholic drink and then subsequently having an accident (in practice I'm not sure how this would work out, but I have read a lot of policy statements that indicate even one glass could void the company from paying out).

- Health: They don't cover STIs (and hey, always wear a condom). If you do have health issues, you must disclose them at the time of booking. This will affect the premium.

- Check the 'dangerous activities' section. Even driving a motorbike in some countries (or being a passenger on one) voids your travel insurance. So check the activities you may want to do and decide if not having insurance for those activities is worth it, or investigate a different type of insurance (and add it as an extra if possible).

- Check the 'general exclusions' section. For example, if you decide to ride a moped in Asia and you don't have a motorbike license back home, you will not be paid out for any accidents you may have. That could be very costly.

I know I sound like a nerd, but I have downloaded and read many insurance Product Disclosure Statements, confirming that basically most insurance companies can get out of paying you anything. So I choose the best out of the lot and the ones that seemed a bit more flexible and cover the things that are important to me: a decent payout for my camera and computer.

Money

Gone are the days when travelers checks were the currency of choice for transacting overseas. I've traveled for the last 6 years without a single one! The truth is, I wouldn't even begin to know where and how to use one.

I have traveled all over South America, Asia, Europe, UK, USA and some of Africa just using my ATM card. Even in Myanmar, which is only just opening up to tourists, I was able to withdraw from ATMs (which are increasing in numbers across the country).

I have back up credit cards (hidden in different places in my luggage, so if one gets lost or stolen, I have back up elsewhere).

When I arrive at a country, I withdraw cash directly from an ATM at the airport. This saves both time and money. I avoid fees and changeable rates at a currency exchange business. Then I withdraw money in the country when I need it. Towards the end of my trip I try and minimize left over currency which I exchange as I'm leaving, if required.

Card fees

It is worthwhile investigating how much your bank charges you for withdrawals and purchases on your cards. Some banks have exorbitant exchange rates and ATM withdrawal fees. What I do:

- An online search for 'best cards to take whilst traveling overseas'.
- Find a comparison site for the various card rates and fees.
- Find the card that I'm able to use in the countries I visit (for me that's globally - I have both a Visa and MasterCard Debit card which means I can use Visa and

MasterCard facilities all over the world using my money and not credit, which is better for me long term, but if you're on short term holidays, using your credit card might work just fine).

- I sign up with the bank that has minimal or no ATM fees (some in country banks charge you for withdrawing money which is extra to any fees your bank may charge you) and good exchange rates.

Driving overseas

Check the country laws where you will be traveling to (by looking on an embassy site or even looking online at car rental companies in the country) and find out whether they require an international driving license. I have never needed an international driving license and have used my country's driving license wherever I've gone. If you do need an international driving license, get onto it as soon as possible as government processes can take a while.

Phones

Should you take your phone overseas? 98% of travelers I've met have a smartphone. I recommend traveling with a smartphone (even if it's a few years old, I've traveled with my 3GS for 5 years and it has been a lifesaver on many occasions).

Do you need to purchase an abroad phone package before you leave? Unless you are on a business trip I think it is completely unnecessary. You can connect to wifi to communicate with your friends and family back home (and use free calling apps like

Skype). Also, it is infinitesimally cheaper to buy a local sim card when you arrive. If I'm in a country for a length of time I purchase a sim card so I can communicate with local friends or make local calls.

Researching ways to get there

Firstly, I want to pay homage to the wonders of the internet. Travel has literally transformed in the last decade through instant access to booking hotels, transport, restaurants and information about places all over the world.

In saying this however, although Wi-Fi is readily accessible all over the world, you can't bank on having access every time you need it. For example, even though most airports I've traveled to offer free Wi-Fi, there are actually a couple I've found that charge you for Wi-Fi and you need to have a local phone number to use the Wi-Fi service. If you don't have a local number, you can't confirm your details and therefore can't use the Wi-Fi. I've also been to airports that don't have computers to access the internet either. I've been caught out several times.

Outside of airports, I've gone out of my way to get to coffee shops with Wi-Fi and the Wi-Fi has been down. This has happened when I've most needed it.

I have been saved a few times by having addresses and numbers already researched and written down in my notebook (or in my smart phone). With no Wi-Fi, back up plans are invaluable.

Realistically, when you arrive in a country, more often than not, you won't have roaming internet on your phone. You will need to get transport to where you are staying and you are unlikely to have wifi in this transport. Even if you have organized a driver, what if she/he doesn't show up? You will need the details of your hotel and alternative means to get there. I recently arrived at a major international airport and their Wi-Fi was down the whole hour or so I was there.

Word: Doing your research beforehand and writing it down will mean you have a room to sleep in!

Flight investigations

More often than not, the cheapest option to get to your next destination is to fly. There are so many possibilities when it comes to flying and the multitudes of online travel agents are a testament to this. It is super easy to book a cheap flight in a manner of minutes using an online travel agent.

There are numerous travel booking websites you can use that help you determine the easiest, cheapest way to get from one place to another. It's a bonus if you can get it all on one site. It is worth checking the site out to see how aggregated and broad their research into local and international travel options are. I often cross reference the travel options with info from online forums such as TripAdvisor or Lonely Planet. One site I recently found out about is Rome2Rio. It is a fairly comprehensive site that has built in options for dozens of multiple transport alternatives (and includes comparable prices for train, bus or plane, which I find is a good start for deeper research).

The primary site I use to research flights is skyscanner.net. It compares multiple online travel agencies and airlines for the best prices. The first thing I check after cost is travel time. Often, it is better to pay an extra $20 to halve the flight time (it constantly surprises me that often the second or fourth cheapest option means 40 hours of traveling). Of course there are other flight searching sites that you will become familiar with and may prefer to use. The amount of time you spend researching various options can be short or endless. When I first started researching flights, I would spend days trying to get the best deal for the quickest time. These days, I generally stick to one of the flight searching travel sites (essentially to save time), check out the various options and book. I'd rather spend my time on other things. However, the choice is yours.

TIP: Use a 'private browser' when you are searching flights. I find it remarkable how all travel sites, airlines and booking companies remember what you were looking for and all of a sudden, your flights have increased in price the following day (it probably isn't that remarkable, since all companies use cookies to understand your buying patterns). If you use a 'private browser' less cookies are added onto your searches and the prices are more likely to stay the same over the coming days (there are no guarantees of course - all depends on the numbers of people booking flights over the period, but generally I've found that most prices tend to stay the same or be fairly consistent over a week or so (depending on how far out your flight is of course) using a private browser.

Booking online

The benefits of booking online by yourself are:

- You can get an immediate booking,
- It is simple, fairly straightforward, and
- Often cheap.

What you have to watch out for:

- Penalty fees. If you need to change your booking, often the penalty fees are quite hefty with these online companies.
- Luggage allowance.
- Meals (including meal preferences).
- Special access bookings.

You may not be able to book these when you are making a booking on a third party travel agent site (which could be fourth or fifth party sites depending on who owns the particular online agency). This means that you may need to make a call to the agency post confirmation of your booking and add luggage or special meals. Alternatively, you may need to speak directly to the airline which will cost you extra.

Booking directly with the airline

I prefer to book directly with the airline if I am making an online booking. Going straight to the source I believe is always best. I do this even if it costs me a little extra (my general rule is paying no more than about $20 or $30 above the lowest agency price). It also lessens the muck around and extra fees associated with changing your flights. Depending on the type of flight you book with the airline, you are likely to have flight changing fees direct with the airline, but this is less than it would be if you include the travel agency fees as well as the airline fees.

Also, if the flight is delayed and you are getting a transfer, the airline is likely to look after you better because you are their direct customer. I have had this happen to me a couple of times now. The airline desk attendants have re-booked the flights quickly and easily, advising that this service was due to the fact that I had booked and paid with them directly.

Booking through a travel agent

There are many reasons to book directly with a travel agent, including:

- They search their systems for the best prices for you,
- It's a personalized service & they may request special upgrades for you,
- They take the responsibility for the booking (including if something goes wrong in your travels), and
- It's usually a stress free process.

Nevertheless, there is one reason why booking with a travel agent is the ideal that surpasses all other reasons: they help you if the airline f's up and/or you get stuck somewhere.

The time I made my first overseas trip, I rocked up to the airport to find out the flight was cancelled. My first solo adventure overseas and it had been scratched! I booked my flights through a travel agent. I called her up and she was able to reschedule my flights and hotels. It was such a relief that someone was there to support me. I ended up in a hotel supplied by the airline company and enjoyed a comfortable night before being driven back to the airport (side note: my first travel photo was of my own city outside my hotel window that included a picture of my workplace as the central feature). Although there was a delay of 24 hours to my journey, it went as smoothly as it could. Also, the travel agent claimed all the extra expenses from my travel insurance for me. It could not have been easier!

Changing your flights on your own initiation is also simpler. Just send your agent an email or give them a call and they'll change it all for you in a flash (often quicker than an airline can).

It is worth noting that travel agents generally get paid through commissions with the airlines/ tour companies etc. Most do not charge extra fees on top of your flights / accommodation bookings etc. Some might charge extra, and it's worth finding that out at the start (I understand some travel agents charge for their time, but if you end up booking with them, they drop the fee).

Train & bus bookings

The options for booking train and bus travel are pretty similar to that of flights:

- Booking through a travel agency.
- Booking online through a travel agency.

- Booking directly through the train or bus lines (online, phone or in person).

They have fairly similar issues and outcomes for each. The main difference is that usually luggage weight and the amount of luggage is a lot greater (for long distances). However, that is not always the case as some train, bus and also ferry companies have a baggage amount limit. It is always worth checking!

Preparation for your departure

This is perhaps one of the most stressful times, preparing for travel. There is usually so much to do and organize at home before you go (including paying bills so that things are still connected when you get back) and at work, prior to your break. Then there is the question of what to pack. This is the one I hope to help you out with in the following chapter, aptly titled 'Get Packed!'.

A quick checklist for before you leave home:

- ✔ All bills up to date?
- ✔ Home looked after? (plants being watered, mail brought in etc.)
- ✔ Companion animals cared for?
- ✔ Are things essentially clean and in order (there is nothing worse than coming home to a pile of laundry when what you need is a clean pair of underwear, pyjamas and a fresh towel)?

✔ Spare key given to a neighbor, friend or family member?

✔ If you are going for a longer period, you may consider mail re-direction to a trusted person to open your mail for you (or change your address to your trusted person's place before you go), you may be moving out, in which case there is a lot more work including putting your stuff in storage, finalizing any paperwork associated with the home and cutting off essential services to your residence including water, electricity etc. Good luck with all of that. I've been there a few times and it's all-consuming.

Before leaving work:

✔ Told your boss? (joking of course, but this is kinda essential!)

✔ Put a redirect on your emails and an out-of-office automatic reply?

✔ Brought in a celebratory cake? (you either want to rub it in or share the holiday joy around - take your pick!).

Personal preparations

Health on the Road

When I embarked on my first trip I was ultra-prepared. Doctor visits, Homeopath, Naturopath and sup'd up on drugs from the Chemist. I mean, I had everything from your garden variety drugs to little pill homeopath specials.

Now I don't see a doctor unless it's part of a visa requirement. For example, when I traveled to South America, I had to have a Yellow Fever injection as part of my entry and exit requirements. I now only travel with the essential drugs that I've listed in the following chapter 'Get Packed!'.

Most countries are less chaotic than they're made out to be and as long as you are careful, (i.e. don't drink local water where it isn't safe to drink), only eat street food that is known to be good and safe, and get your digestive enzymes working, you should be ok. For example, when I was in India, I ordered a lassi with every meal. A lassi contains yogurt which has all the good bacteria to support gut health. You can also take pro-biotic pills for the journey.

If you do need to have any vaccinations, you need to plan months ahead of your trip, as some only start working after certain periods of time, others you need a series of injections. Consult your doctor or specialist travel doctor in your area.

Medications

The truth is, there are pharmacies everywhere. The only issue is potential language barriers to communicate effectively and getting the specific products you require. Some medications are prescription based. If you are traveling to remote locations, doing a trek or something similar you may want to travel with a basic first aid kit. You can pick them up in travel stores. Or you can just get the basics of what you think you may need for your toiletries bag.

I simply carry a separate small toiletry bag with the basic stuff I think I might need: burn cream, papaya ointment/antiseptic cream, Band-Aids, antiseptic gel, diarrhea stoppers, rehydration satchels and headache pills. You may want to carry more or less. I believe the most essential travel item is diarrhea stoppers. The worst thing in my opinion is being caught with the runs right before a long travel day. I'm not a massive fan of medication, but I am quite happy to pop one of these at the slightest discomfort. Avoiding rancid bus or train toilets, I will do at any cost.

If you do have prescriptions, make sure you also carry a letter from your doctor stating that they are for your personal medicinal use. Sometimes customs officials are a bit funny about some medications (particularly if you are traveling with an amount of stuff).

Personal care products

If you are only traveling for a week or two, you may feel comfortable using basic traveling products that you can buy from a chemist or in your local supermarket (the cute small travel products are wonderful). What I also love are the empty containers and tubes that you can buy in travel stores which you can fill with your favorite products. These travel tubes / containers are plastic and, importantly, light.

For longer travel, I have found it necessary to bring my standard products. This often means larger, heavier containers and tubes, but the benefits to me far outweigh the extra weight and space. It means I can have the products that work for me for a good portion of the time. I am fussy, so when I've had to buy products overseas, I have done a lot of research before purchasing (thank the heavens for google translate and the availability of health stores worldwide). I've listed in the next chapter what I usually carry with me.

Computers & cameras

I know many travelers are afraid to take a computer or camera with them on their travels. There are obvious benefits for not taking one or both. It's lighter and less bulky. You don't have to worry about losing them or someone stealing them. If you don't take a computer, you are less likely to spend too much time on the internet.

I own a MacBook Pro and a pretty decent camera. I would not leave home without them. I also travel with other computer equipment including: backup hard disks, a smart phone and an MP3 player. It's heavy, but they are just too important to my enjoyment not to take them. I'm a hobby photographer, and having the computer allows me to upload my pics and save them to backups. A computer allows me to write and work anywhere. It's also much easier using a computer than navigating and responding to stuff on a tiny smartphone.

It depends again on what your purpose is for your holiday. Is it a short break to relax and leave work behind? Forget the computer.

Are high quality photos important to you? No? Just use your smartphone (you'll have to get access to computers to download your pics, or you could just upload them to your email or social media and that may be enough for you).

Exercise

Before I embarked on my first major solo traveling journey, I had been on a 6-month fitness stint, going to the gym every day of the week. I loved it. Especially resistance / weight training. I wasn't sure what would happen when I commenced my journey. I really wanted to continue my regime. But I knew going to the gym at every location (on a budget too) would be highly impossible.

So I turned to what I knew best: research. I wanted to find something portable, but not bulky (I only had a backpack) that I could use anywhere. Of course there are exercise videos on YouTube, which vary in quality and awesomeness, but what if I don't have Wi-Fi in my room? (this has happened a lot - no Wi-Fi in my room).

And what about resistance? After weeks of searching, I found some resistance bands, not the flimsy type, but strong round rubber, suitable for proper resistance and can be carried anywhere. And it came with a DVD. I was set! I have used the same resistance cord/band thing for 5 years (on and off when I've been in different mind frames or spaces). I can use it anywhere and in fairly small spaces. The great thing about the band and the instructional video is that it really works my whole body. It has been so useful for warming up different muscles, stretching them after carrying backpacks; sleeping in bad beds; all day walking; or even a day on the computer. Any niggling complaint (sore shoulders or back pain) goes away. The beauty of a good workout (and even better: it only takes 25 minutes).

You can always jog or run, but some areas are not safe to do so. Most are ok, but the truth is, I've never been a fan of jogging or running. Hats off to those of you who are! Walking is great (and I do a lot of that), but sometimes you need all your muscles stretched. Yoga is another great option.

So you can still get your exercise in, even on the tightest schedule!

Cultural preparations

I strongly recommend preparing yourself, at least in some way for the country you are landing in. Depending on the country, ask yourself these questions:

- What are the major **languages** of the country? (in many countries throughout the world, there will be one or two 'official' languages and then a whole pile of local and indigenous languages).

- How big is the **population**? (knowing whether you are going to a cosmopolitan city which has a variety of people who are likely to have some English speakers or whether you are landing in a small town with not much of either is kinda helpful.

- What do most women and men **wear**? (in many countries locals dress conservatively - respect this and make sure you wear clothes that cover the parts most locals cover e.g. shoulders, stomach, thighs. I will also observe when I arrive what other women wear & I will cover the parts of my body that most local women do. Locals consider this respectful. Particularly important is if you visit places of worship, make sure you always cover up – I wear pants and longer sleeve t-shirts and/or I use a scarf for my arms).

- What are the major **religions**? (Again knowing this will help you in your dressing and also know generally what not to say, e.g. inappropriate jokes).

- What are the main types of **food** (this is not only important because you can start to be excited about what you are going to eat, but also what you need to have a lot of before you leave - so you don't miss it so much when you're there!).

Now all of this shouldn't take you long (a quick Wiki search will give you the very basics, but if you're keen, there will always be much more than this). It's worth doing. Then you don't look like a rabbit in headlights for the first few days of your arrival or make some major faux pas, or worse still land you in police headquarters for making some major cultural no -no.

Language basics

Above all, I recommend learning the language basics. Now I'm not saying you should take a year's worth of language classes before you leave (although if you want to, go for it! Awesome!). But it doesn't take much to learn a few words to make easy friends on your arrival.

The most essential basics

I believe that there are 3 key words / phrases, that if you can learn them in any language, they will take you very far. They have with me.

- Hello!
- Thank you!
- The food is delicious.

If you only learn these 3 phrases in each local language, you will travel easily throughout any country. I speak the truth.

Above the most essential basics

- How are you?
- I am fine / better than good.
- Can I please have…
- A little bit.
- Your shop is lovely!
- Goodbye! Have a nice day!

If you can say this, they will think you can speak the language and you will have gained instant respect.

2 pages and you are completely set

My rule of thumb is to write down a page or two of the language (and I usually do this phonetically as I am hopeless at intonation otherwise). Sometimes I write down what I've found on the internet and then ask a local when I get there how to pronounce it. I have never met anyone not more than willing to explain to me how to pronounce something correctly. Another great way to make instant friends.

For me, I have dietary requirements, so I learn all the words in the language that involves the stuff I can't eat, and then the word 'no' or 'without'.

How to find the language basics

To find the language basics out I usually use the world's most well-known search engine, type in for example 'Moroccan language basics' and it regularly comes up with a few sites that have introductions and the most popular travel phrases.

If you are keen, you can purchase basic language books to use whilst you are there. There are also a multitude of translation apps for most languages. You can download an app before you go. They are incredibly handy to have on your phone and some apps let you search for basic words and translations without Wi-Fi (this is the best if you can find it).

I also regularly use google translate when I'm in a country (its incredibly useful, even if it's not always accurate).

Again, as soon as I arrive, I ask a local how to pronounce the key words (which I find is always different from the phonetical spelling that I've read).

Hot tip!

Learning the words 'No Thank you' in local languages has helped me escape the extremely persistent market sellers / hawkers in many places around the world.

Hawkers tend to be very annoying if I just speak English to them, but they tend to back away almost immediately whenever I use their language.

Of course there is a lot more...

On a completely contradictory note, don't research too much! Leave some exploration room! You will never be able to know everything about a country anyway, and it is ALWAYS different from what you read or imagine. Sometimes attempting to read or research everything about a country could lead to preconceptions... which you may like being challenged, or not!

There will always be a lot that you didn't find out, and there is joy in that.

For the journey

Reading & music material

I remember my best friend at 18, undertaking her first travel to Europe with a portable cassette player and a few very worn mixed tapes.

A few years later, she traveled with a Walkman and an A3 wallet packed full of CDs. It weighed a few kilos. And it was all worth it to have music on the go. Travelers would swap CDs in long bus rides to expand their music horizons.

I remember when she first came back from her trip to Hawaii many years after that and she was so excited, "I've got something to show you that will revolutionize your music."

"Really?"

"Look, it contains all your CDs in this little box. Take it. Have a look." I remember swirling the dial around and flicking through her albums on the tiny screen. It was easy to use. But I was hesitant. This hesitancy was quickly overcome on my purchase of one. So much music and in such a light instrument.

It has really revolutionized travel, along with smartphones. You can do anything with such a small, light device! Usually before I travel, I will review my music collection and maybe download a new album or two to have some new tracks for my longer journeys (knowing that I won't have Wi-Fi on that journey for apps like Spotify). Often there is a defining album that carries me through a particular traveling experience. Go find that album for you.

Books: I've seen many travelers with paperbacks. There are a lot of advantages with paperbacks; that worn smell, being able to flip back a few pages with your hands, fold corners and gaze at the cover. In lots of places (some cafes, accommodation places etc.), you can find books that you can swap with, enabling you to get your next read. The detraction of course is bulk and weight.

Here I am a convert yet again. E-readers for travel are the bomb! Super light, super easy to travel with and you can access 1000 books at your fingertips. What more could you want? If I were to purchase my e-reader again, I would get a backlight, as it's so much easier if you don't have a lamp beside your bed at night or just want to read under the covers.

Snacks

Depending on where you are going & how you will get there:

Always consider bringing snacks. Especially if you have dietary requirements. If you are catching an el-cheapo flight, they are likely to not cater for you on their 'order off the menu' items (and I have found that often menu items are not available). I like being prepared regardless. What if they have run out of things? And don't you want your own special treats anyway?

Always bring water. If you carry your own reusable water bottle like I do, some airports have purified refilling stations after the security check, so you can empty your water first and then refill it once you're at the terminal. This is great, it cuts down plastic consumption, better for you and the environment. And then you can use your refillable bottle on the road. Even in countries where you can't drink the tap water, you can buy 5 litre bottles and refill your reusable water bottle for day out adventures. Also, hotels regularly offer purified water (and even some cafes) for free or for a very reasonable price.

I'm a self-confessed food addict, and I hope I'm not alone in thinking it vital that you consider snacks when planning your travel. Many factors will need to determine your level of preparation for this one:

- Type of travel
- Length of travel and
- Mode of travel

Snacks & the length of travel

If you are going on a couple of hours' flight from Amsterdam to Venice, you may only need to pack a few snacks, peanuts, a bar of chocolate and the like. If you are traveling further afield let's say from Oslo to Bangkok, one may need to pack a few more things... for example: chips, 4 bars of chocolate, a protein bar, mix nuts, a sandwich, piece of cake, to name a few.

I've been known to take a full grocery bag of snacks for long haul flights (I'm not kidding - an extra carry-on bag full of nibbles and my neck pillow). Now I understand that on most long haul flights they provide food, but one can never be too sure. Ever.

Snacks & the type of travel

You could be on a 4 hour el cheapo flight from London to Istanbul or a 6 midnight special Brisbane to Bali stint. The truth is, you could probably survive without food for this length of time, but not me. Me without food is not a pretty sight. I become hollowed and haunted, a mere saliva drop emanating from a pig's mouth in a muddy yard.

If you are the type that flies first class, you probably don't have to worry too much about this, as you will be fed. Well, lucky you. But for my friends who may not be so fortuitous, this is for you!

For those catching el cheapo flights, where meals must be paid for in flight, be careful if you have dietary requirements because they are regularly not catered for on the in-flight menu.

Snacks & the mode of travel

The mode of travel is important, because if you're on a plane, you receive snacks at scheduled times and that is it. You are not able to just pop out and get something. Whereas with bus travel generally they have scheduled stops and food is always available at these stops. Depending on the train company, generally there is a food carriage where you can order stuff. And this is a very good thing.

Finally, I want to share with you a story about being prepared...

When I commenced a year long journey into the unknown, I had booked and paid for a taxi transfer and hotel in Bangkok, Thailand, for the first week of my stay. I had never been to Thailand before. It was a nice hotel. I knew I needed a few days to recover from the very busy schedule I'd had in the months prior to departure, and I thought a nice hotel, close to the vibrant Koh Sahn Road and a good Thai massage options would do the trick.

I triple checked and printed out my transfer details from the airport to the hotel and had backup plans if the driver did not show up. I even had a backup hotel (just in case my booking went astray or something), printed it out for 'just in case' (and no, I didn't think it was over the top at the time, just practical, everyone would do that right?).

I landed for a short stopover in Kuala Lumpur at the 'el cheapo' AirAsia terminal full of plastic 70s decor, doing its best to moderate the humidity with its similar age technology outbursts, a few random stalls that looked like we were eating off local street vendors. After 72 hours of no sleep, it was a little challenging for me to negotiate (side note: thankfully this terminal has been completely upgraded in 2015 to a haven of gourmet restaurants, sassy shops and comfortable lounges).

I managed to log into Wi-Fi at the only place selling the only thing that could keep me awake. As I logged onto Facebook, I noticed some panicked messages from my friends. Reports from

Bangkok: flooding had become substantially worse and most of the city, including some airports, were cut off. My inner dialogue went something like this:

Shit. What the f' am I going to do now?

I've already booked my hotel and airport transfer, but what if they can't get to the airport? What will I do then? I could stay at the airport I guess, but I presume a lot of people are and it's likely to be full. And it's likely to be very expensive. And it's not the ambient start to my holiday I was expecting. Damn.

I went back to check the board and flight details. It told me there was a delay due to rain. I decided to line up with a long line of people to ask what everyone else I guessed was asking: was the plane still flying into Bangkok?

"Yes we are."

"Ok."

I logged back online to attempt to find out more information. *I was planning to visit Siem Reap after Bangkok, maybe I could go straight there?*

I checked flights - none leaving that night. A new thought emerged. *I could always stay in Kuala Lumpur and then catch a flight in a few days to Siem Reap. It was late and dark, but surely I could get a hotel for a night in town and work it out from there?*

In my sleep deprived haze (I had not slept in 72 hours), I walked back to the airline desk and asked if I could remove my bag. They said I would need to ask at another desk about 100 meters away. I went to where they described, but I couldn't find anyone. I walked back. A man appeared and I asked whether it was possible.

"I am not sure, the plane is already scheduled to depart. I'll ask."

After about 15 minutes, he returned. "What does your bag look like?"

"It's a black backpack."

"Ok." He disappeared again. I was not sure if I was supposed to wait or go. I kept looking around for what seemed 20 minutes, but was probably 5.

After some time, another man appeared. "Come with me."

"What about my backpack?"

"It will be upstairs waiting for you." *Oh no, I don't want to lose my luggage on my first flight!*

I followed him through a maze of stairs and corridors until we reached a small office.

"This girl was flying to Bangkok, but now wants to stay here."

It was all smiles and laid back questions whilst my visa was stamped and I was ushered out.

"Your bag will be over there."

I looked in vain in the direction he pointed as he quickly disappeared down a passage way behind me. I hesitantly moved to where he gestured. Sure enough, on approaching a closed random door, my backpack was sitting there.

I jumped my backpack on. *I can do this, right?* I walked out and looked for an information counter. Luckily, everyone spoke excellent English. I had no idea what language was even spoken in Kuala Lumpur, what country it was a part of, or even if it was its own country like Hong Kong.

On finding out that the airport hotels were way out of my budget, I asked what a taxi price would be into town.

"About 90 Ringgit."

I had no idea what the exchange rate was, but it sounded like a lot.

"Are there any cheaper options to get into town?"

"You can catch a bus by walking out the terminal to the left and getting on any bus there."

"Ok, thank you." *I know 'Kop kun Kaa' in Thai, but that's not relevant here. What language do they speak here? And how do I say 'thank you' in their language?*

I made my way out into the thick air-watered evening, attempting to follow the directions along a dimly lit path.

"You come here."

"Okay. The city?"

I found my way towards the back of the dingy bus. Pulling my heavy front pack onto my lap I watched the unlit space slowly fill up over the next 30 minutes. *10.30pm. God I hope there is some hotel open when it gets into town. Surely there will be one open - I've heard this is a big city.*

I strained to spot any other white faces I could connect with. I could see none. *It's going to be okay. There is sure to be something open. Hopefully close to the bus stop.*

The vacant but bright bus terminal, an hour later showed not a hotel in sight. Nothing. *Damn. I'll have to ask. God, I'm so tired.*

Stepping off the bus, I looked around. *I don't even know where to go. Or who to ask that I can trust.* Spotting some other backpacks about 20 meters away, I moved to try and make eye contact. I smiled. It looked like they were just about to get into a taxi. *I can go wherever they are going. That's it.*

"Hi! Can I share a ride with you guys?"

"Sure, where are you going?"

"I'm hoping to go to a cheap hotel somewhere."

"Well there are some around where I am going, jump in."

My sense of relief was overwhelming.

"I normally stay in this little place where I get my own room but share a bathroom. They may have more rooms available, if not, there will be plenty of other options in the same strip."

"Great."

…

I have shared this story with you, because even though you can prepare as much as you can, shit happens. Circumstances beyond your control often occurs when you're traveling. Being prepared is one thing, and it helps you understand what you need to do if something unplanned happens. There is however a deep, rich satisfaction when you see how you respond to stressful situations and realize you can survive, and you do!

However, being prepared gets you in the right frame of mind and understanding of what you need to make your travel as smooth and easy as possible.

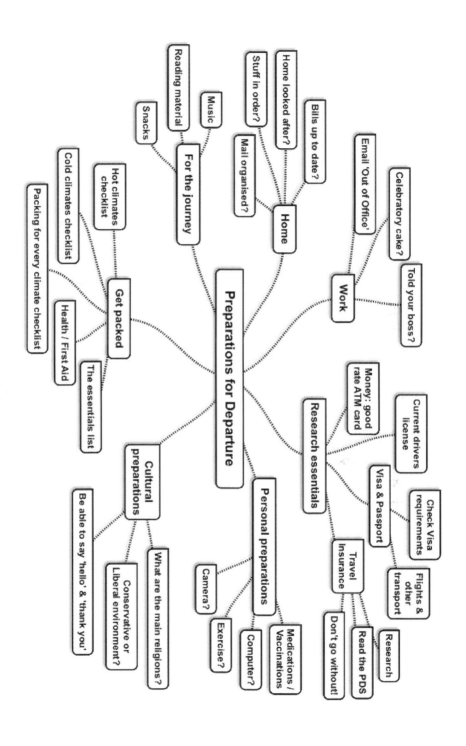

Preparations for Departure

For the journey
- Reading material
- Music
- Snacks

Home
- Stuff in order?
- Home looked after?
- Mail organised?
- Bills up to date?

Work
- Email 'Out of Office'
- Celebratory cake?
- Told your boss?

Get packed
- Cold climates checklist
- Hot climates checklist
- Packing for every climate checklist
- Health / First Aid
- The essentials list

Research essentials
- Money: good rate ATM card
- Current drivers license
- Visa & Passport
- Check Visa requirements
- Flights & other transport

Cultural preparations
- Be able to say 'hello' & 'thank you'
- Conservative or Liberal environment?
- What are the main religions?

Personal preparations
- Camera?
- Exercise?
- Computer?
- Medications / Vaccinations

Travel Insurance
- Don't go without!
- Read the PDS
- Research

3. Get packed!

Packing can be daunting, but it also can be fun! It means you might have to purchase new items (if you love shopping, that's great!) or you may want to travel with a virtually empty case and fill up on exotic things as you go. This chapter is all about what you will need for the majority of trips (for specialty adventure trips such as skiing or biking, you'll have to create your own list for these things, but this is for everything else).

What to pack:

The first questions:

- How long are you going for?
- Will you just be traveling in the same type of climate for the length of your travels? (i.e. just hot and humid or cold and snowy).
- Will you have a combination of temperatures? (even if you are in a hot environment, sometimes it will still get cold at night).
- Do you need to take any specialist equipment? (i.e. for hobbies or sport - a tripod or mountain gear for example).

Fire up your favorite search engine or Wikipedia and type in the name of your country / city and weather forecasts. You will find out the details of the average temperatures for each month of the year and most importantly, rainfall averages. This will help determine your packing requirements.

I've found that if you are packing for 5 days, a couple of weeks, months, or years, I pretty much take about the same amount of stuff.

I've listed the below as a starter for you to consider for your main bag/suitcase/backpack. At the end of this chapter I have listed everything I carry in my 'front pack' or carry-on bag and have separated out these lists intentionally. You will need to separate your luggage as well, and this will provide you with some initial guidance.

Obviously each woman's needs differ, for example I don't wear glasses or contact lenses. I take a little bit of makeup and I know some women take none or a whole compartment full of it. So take the below lists and modify them to suit your needs. It's a beginning point for your bag packing adventure!

The bare essentials

Toiletries:

I find toiletry bags from travel shops the best for packing these essentials:

- Toothbrush.
- Toothpaste.

- Floss.

- Mouthwash.

- Shampoo & Conditioner.

- Hair products.

- Face cream.

- Under eye cream.

- Body oil or cream.

- Face cleanser & sponge.

- Soap and soap container.

- Exfoliation gloves.

- Make up.

- Nail file, nail buffer, nail cutter, tweezers.

- Deodorant.

- Small perfume bottle.

You may want to condense the above list, depending on your preference. Most airports and local supermarkets stock shampoo, conditioner, toothbrushes and toothpaste etc. I have listed the above because I like taking my preferred products from home (that I know I can't get elsewhere).

Health stuff:

I carry the below in another toiletry bag I bought from a travel shop:

- Band-Aids.

- Tea tree oil (or your fav all-purpose antiseptic solution).

- Papaw ointment (or your fav cleansing / rash relieving cream).

- Burn aid.

- Diarrhea stop tablets.

- Rehydration satchels.

- Vitamin C & B Complex (one always needs a hangover cure!).

- Tampons & panty liners. I also carry a few pads, as I prefer them - but you can buy pads everywhere (but not always tampons).

- Condoms.

Useful items:

- Swiss army knife (they come in many sizes and no woman should travel without one - this must be packed in your main luggage otherwise it will be confiscated).

- Spork (incredibly handy if you need to eat on the run - pick one up at your local travel shop).

- Sewing repair kit (for those random rips and button pops! I have a couple of different types of thread and some sewing needles and that's it).

- Light (can use one on your phone if you have it, but it's useful to have a spare light or head torch - I've surprised myself how useful head torches are - even if they look incredibly dodgy).

- Spare batteries (if you are traveling with anything that uses batteries).

- Rain covers for your big or smaller backpacks (buy in travel shops).
- A universal travel adaptor.
- A small laundry line (bought from a travel shop - very useful for drying clothes in small spaces) and laundry soap bar (lasts a long time).

Underwear:

This depends on how long you are going for. I keep my underwear and socks in separate zipped up bra bags (which then become useful for washing in your travels). Generally, I take:

- 10 pairs of underwear.
- 2 normal bras and 1 sports bra.
- 3 pairs of socks.
- 6 pairs of sockets.

For hot climates:

- A sarong. A sarong is always the first thing I pack (but they are cheap, so you can always pick one up if you are heading to southeast Asia).
- Thongs / flip flops.
- Sunscreen.
- Hat.
- A pair of shorts (or two).
- A skirt (or two).

- A dress (or two).

- Bathers.

- T-shirts or tops (I have at least 5, sometimes in humid climates you need to change your top a couple of times a day or at least when you go out to dinner at night, you don't want the same sweaty number you wore during the day).

- A going out top (or two. A dress may suffice for this - your preference of course. I usually have at least one top and one dress I would wear for heading out on the town).

Even for hot climates always have:

- A scarf or light jumper or jacket for cool evenings.

- A raincoat and small umbrella, (you can buy umbrellas and plastic rain sheets in local stores wherever you go, but I like having it prepared before I leave).

For cold climates:

- A beanie.

- Gloves.

- A Scarf or two (one can never have enough scarves and they dress up any outfit!).

- Two pairs of pants (you can get travel shop ones, jeans and/or also have a dressier pair).

- A belt (if required).

- Two long sleeve shirts.

- A warm jacket and a wind protector jacket.

- Thermals (top and bottom).

- Solid shoes.

- I usually have at least one top and jacket for 'going out' purposes. Usually you can get away with everyday pants if you have a nice top. It's all in the top really!

If you're into exercise:

- Light runners.

- Sweat pants/shorts.

- Exercise shirt & sports bra (I take one sports bra, but if you're highly energetic, you may want to take two and alternate).

A word on laundry when you travel. If you are traveling to SE Asian / South American countries, you will find it's relatively cheap to get your laundry washed, dried and folded (sometimes pressed even!). Occasionally underwear may go missing, so if you like any particular underwear, wash it yourself. In other places, you may want to wash your clothes yourself (I get into a routine of hand washing at night and letting it drip dry using my travel shop laundry line). I've hand washed all my clothes for months at a time (the longest was a 6-month period), and they turn out just fine.

What if you need to prepare for any weather eventuality?

Essentially I travel with everything I will need for most climates (because I travel for years at a time). That sounds like a lot, but let me break it down for you. This is what I travel with (I am constantly amazed how much continues to fit in my backpack!).

For the cooler climates:

- One Singlet Thermal.
- One long sleeve black Thermal (this can double as an extra-long sleeve shirt - or you can wear under another shirt).
- One long Thermal pants.
- Two corduroy pants (or you could do jeans -whatever your preference).
- A belt (if required).
- Two pairs of tights and one pair of leggings (leggings can also replace pants - as they are less bulky).
- One pair of very thick socks (doubles as slippers).
- Beanie and gloves.
- 3 scarves.

For the warmer climates:

- A sarong (or 2).
- Thongs / flip flops.

- Bathers.

- Sunscreen and hat.

- Two skirts.

- Two dresses.

- One bike pant (to avoid chub-rub in hot climates - nothing worse than red raw rashes between your thighs from sweat and walking. I love skirts and thin, airy bike pants underneath make it all doable).

For general:

- One comfy jacket type thing (which I always carry with my hand luggage - can double as a blanket or cushion).

- One going out rain jacket (folds up really small).

- Five t-shirts.

- Two going out shirts.

- Two normal bras and 1 sports bra.

- I pair of light pyjamas (ok, ok, so unnecessary, but I like hanging out in my PJs! And if I'm staying with people, it's comfortable). For cooler climates, I just wear my jumper/jacket type thing over the top of my PJs, which works perfectly.

- 10 pairs of underwear, 4 pairs of socks, 6 sockets.

- One solid pair of travel shoes (that I do everything in, literally: going out, hiking, meandering about).

- One very light pair of exercise runners.

- One sweatpants & top.

- One exercise band.

Layering for changes in weather obviously helps. I wear my t-shirts all the time, and if it's a cooler day, I'll wear a short or long sleeve thermal underneath, which works really well.

If you are traveling for a lengthier period of time (6 months, a year or two) you will find that some clothes actually start to get holes in (who would have thought?). When I'm home living in Australia, I rarely find my clothes develop holes (well not within 6 months usually) and I quite like that feeling of really using an item before I need to replace it. I regularly sew holes up whilst on the road and see how long that lasts.

If I'm in the mood for a new top (after all, wearing the same clothes day in and out for 6 months sometimes you just want to have something fresh), I will make myself give away one item for every new item purchased. I've tried to grow my backpack and fit more and more in, but I have found, after dedicated practice, a limit.

My front pack:

My front pack (that I carry on my back for day trips when I'm not carrying my large backpack for travel) contains all my necessary pleasure tools: camera, computer, phone etc. As you will gather, it is a decent sized front pack (travel shop bought) with many sections to organize and stash the following items:

- Sunglasses in a case.
- Big plastic rain sheet (when pulled out it easily goes over me & my front pack).

- My front pack rain cover (specifically designed for small backpacks).

- Small umbrella.

- My travel essentials in a little plastic bag (all under 100ml to go through any airport security scanner): hand gel, deodorant, hand wipes, facial wipes, face cream, tissues, lip balm, pawpaw ointment, small hair oil, small sunscreen).

- Eye mask and earplugs (absolutely essential for all overnight travel anywhere).

- My computer, camera and chargers.

- Universal travel adapters.

- My smartphone, ear phones & e-reader (all charged up and ready to rock).

- My 2 back up hard drives (no, I'm not excessive or anything).

- My passport pouch containing my passport, ATM cards, driver's license, keys, money and travel insurance details.

- An exercise book. Papers and information on my travel, phone numbers and transfer information to my next destination.

- Pens, padlock, nail buffer, ear plugs, eye cover, a couple of Band-Aids, diarrhea stoppers & rehydration satchel, headache tablets, small pack of cards, 3 panty liners, 2 condoms.

- 2 Reusable shopping bags (both fold into the size of a mobile phone).

- Lip balm, lighter (which maybe confiscated at customs - depending on the country), notepad.

As you may have guessed, my front pack is quite heavy. And I understand this would be too much for most people. I do recommend traveling light (it's just easier and more comfortable). For me, these items are necessary for everything I want to do, so I will put up with the heaviness, sweat and awkwardness for my greater goal. Again work out what you want to achieve for your trip and pack with this vision in mind.

Packing Checklist

- ✔ Got your passport, flight bookings, itineraries, accommodation details & transfer details, travel insurance, driver's license, ATM cards and money?

- ✔ Got chargers for electronic devices & travel adapters?

- ✔ Got your fav electronic devices charged and ready to rock?

- ✔ Any essential maps and information saved in your phone?

- ✔ Got the relevant language app downloaded on your smartphone?

- ✔ Got useful items (see above list): Swiss army knife (in your checked in luggage) & spork?

- ✔ Sewing kit (in your checked in luggage)?

- ✔ Undies?

- ✔ Shoes?

- ✔ Sunnies, sunscreen, flip flops, hat?

- ✔ Swimmers (you never know when there may be an opportunity to get wet)?

- ✔ Got it all organized at home (see chapter 'Preparation, Preparation, Preparation')?

- ✔ Eye mask and earplugs?

- ✔ Snacks?

- ✔ Umbrella and/or rain protecter?

- ✔ Key to get back in at home (completely optional of course)?

4. Beds and where to sleep

Accommodation options wherever you go are just about endless: From luxury villas, standard hotels, home stays, apartments, renting rooms in homes, flash-packers, to very low budget dorms.

Hotels

One of the major issues in booking a hotel you don't know anything about, especially if you are booking at the cheap end of the market, is the very real concern you will end up in a dive with rats and bed lice waking you at 3.27am whilst the walls shake from your neighbors and sirens sound outside your window because it was not the 'quiet end of town' as promised.

One site that I have found to be enormously useful is TripAdvisor. Anyone can sign up and place a review on this site. I regularly review places I've stayed and eaten at. I like to contribute to this site because it's been so useful to me in working out places to be avoided or those worth checking out. One bad review doesn't put me off, (depending on how reasonable the reviewer appears to be), but I look at a few to gauge an overall feel of the place.

Scoring a deal

There are many websites that offer deals on hotels. What I've noticed is that these 'deals' are often not any better than the prices you find on the hotel's own website. This is especially true when you factor in the extra fees that many of these sites add in at the end when you enter your credit card details.

One option, which I have successfully done, is to find out the specials on the countless conglomerate hotel websites and then go in person to the hotel and negotiate a better deal based on the specials I've seen advertised online. I usually run with 'I saw the room advertised for this price, what offer can you make me now, so that we both avoid the third party fees?' Alternatively, you could call or email the hotel for any direct booking promotions they may have.

It worked recently in a hotel I stayed at in Myanmar. When the hotel owner was not prepared to negotiate, I said that was absolutely fine and asked her to get me a taxi to another hotel (that just so happened to have higher ratings on TripAdvisor), and she all of a sudden decided to negotiate with me! So I ended up with my first preference hotel.

Another option is to book a first night in a central place, then check out the hotel options in the area and negotiate a deal in person. It all depends on whether you want to spend the time doing this, but an advantage is that you get to check out a room before you stay.

Both an attraction and detraction to hotels is the general solitary nature of them. If you want space by yourself, you can walk in and head straight to your room. If you want to talk to people, unless there is a breakfast area or other seating area where travelers gather it's harder to do. I've found people are less likely to strike up conversations in hotels as they would do in hostels. But if you are happy doing your own thing, then this is for you. Generally, hotels are quieter too!

A few of the accommodation sites that you could start with:

- kayak.com
- trivago.com
- momondo.com
- hotelquickly.com
- skyscanner.net
- agoda.com (predominantly for the Asian region)
- hotelscombined.com
- hotels.com
- booking.com
- Another option worth considering is booking through companies like Quidco or Topcashback for up to 12% cashback on sites like hotels.com and booking.com.
- Some people use the forums on reddit and other expat sites to find current deals.

Hostels

Hostels vary dramatically in quality, features and price. Some can be as fancy as hotels with better features and friendlier vibes. Hostels, although generally relegated to young folk, have such a range of people and ages that it can't just be pigeon holed for those under 25. I've met 80 year olds staying in hostels, and they are some of the coolest people I've met!

Again, to work out the vibe of a hostel I check out their website, reviews and always TripAdvisor. Generally, I like to stay in private rooms in hostels (because I like sleep!). Sometimes the private rooms can cost more than hotel rooms (because they calculate the room booking on the number of people per room and usually the private rooms are for 2 people). The benefits of a hostel is that generally you can cook or prepare light snacks in the communal kitchen or enjoy entertainment spaces, which are often very comfortable and nice.

Some hostels cater specifically for the 'flash-packer' market and can be even more expensive than hotels. They provide sparkling, comfortable rooms, spaces to sleep and to be seen.

Hostels are also generally better at knowing about the fun activities and day trips or tours you can take in the location. This is a big benefit.

To start your research for hostels:

If it is high season, it is advisable to book in advance, but outside busy periods, there are possibilities of walking into a hostel and negotiating a deal in person (or book a first night and haggle after this). Again, it's a way to check out a hostel in advance to see if you like it.

- hostelworld.com

- hostelbookers.com
- hostelz.com

Many of the hostel booking sites have reviews from people that have booked and stayed through using the particular booking site. I read the reviews left on this site and compare the reviews with TripAdvisor if I'm unsure.

B&Bs

BnBs are great. You are often in a warm, comfortable home, usually with a good bed and the next morning a hearty breakfast. The majority of the time you get interactions with the host (s) and tips about making your stay special. I've haven't stayed at a lot of B&Bs generally because: they are more expensive than other places I've stayed; sometimes there are shared bathrooms; and regularly they are not in the location of a place I want to explore. As most of my city exploration is by foot, I try and get a place as close into the center of town or the best sites as I can.

There are many specific B&B websites that you can search for specific features and see reviews. Again, TripAdvisor is good to cross reference reviews.

Airbnb

I don't know many people who don't know about Airbnb these days. Airbnb is a global accommodation site that enables homeowners to rent out private or shared rooms in their homes, their entire house or apartment. Homeowners and prospective renters create a profile on Airbnb with a description of themselves, info about the space and the area the home is situated. Both homeowners and renters can write reviews for each other, which enables the owners to assess (along with the profile information) if the person is suitable to stay. Importantly for prospective guests, reviews on the homeowner and space are critical to determine if you want to stay. I never stay with people without good reviews. I also get a feel of a homeowner through emailing them and asking them questions. How they respond to me enables me to make a clear decision on whether to stay with them or not.

I have stayed in amazing places through Airbnb! And I have met some wonderful people. People I've stayed connected with for years later and I still consider them good friends. I like staying in people's homes. They are generally very comfortable; you can usually use the kitchen to cook and often you get to learn a bit about the place through the hosts. I personally could not ask for more when I stay in new places.

Private apartments

There are oodles of private accommodation sites where owners either let their homes and apartments through the site or through agents. I am a big fan of staying in apartments, particularly when I am traveling with someone else (making it very economical). I love having a kitchen when I travel and also my own space to hang out in is more than wonderful after a day of traipsing around.

Again, I check any reviews and I make an assessment about the place through my communication with the owners. I've never had a bad experience using these common sense methods.

Home-stays

In majority world countries, home-stays provide local people with an income, particularly at the times of the year when their crops are sparse. These can be really valuable experiences in learning how other people live, and you may gain a better insight into the culture. I've always done home-stays through ethical tour companies, where I am more confident that the money is being distributed appropriately throughout the communities.

I have always stayed with families that have not spoken any English. It has truly made me a convert to body language being the universal tool for communication. I'm always astounded about the basic things that can be said / communicated without words. We are so heavily reliant on words but you can read so much through facial expression, body language and vocal intonation.

Most people can assess when someone is experiencing big emotions: anger, sadness and joy. Even when you don't know the specifics, these type of emotions are common throughout cultures. Sometimes people demonstrate in different ways, but the fundamentals I've found to be consistent.

Boats

On searching a particular town I wanted to stay in, I found the cheapest accommodation being offered was on a boat. I only had one night there, but it was a fantastic experience learning a little about life on a boat and the boating communities.

Couchsurfing

Finally, a word on Couchsurfing. For those not familiar with Couchsurfing, it's an international website that is fundamentally about cutting the boundaries between cultures and enabling people to share experiences and time through being hosted in cities they are traveling to. Hosts provide a bed, a room or a couch in their home for free.

Nothing is expected in return, but it is good practice to offer to cook a meal (hosts usually want a dish from your country as it is all about cross cultural exchange / learning), bring something or take the host out for a meal. Different hosts will have different capacities (due to work / other commitments etc.) to show you around the city, take you out on the town, eat together etc. It is all about communication before and whilst you are there.

Generally, hosts will not want to host you for more than a couple of nights (as they are providing accommodation for free), but on the rare occasion it can be longer.

I have found a wide variety of people both host and surf. Although there are a lot of people in their 20s, there are also many in their 30s, 40s and 50s (and there are a few I've met in their 60s plus). Some families host people to introduce their children to different cultures and ways of life.

A word on safety. On exploring the couchsurfing website, you will start to see how varying people's profiles are, their level of completeness and types of reviews. I have a fully completed profile, reviews from hosts (which are just as important for hosts - reviews work both ways) and I've also had my identity verified. I only consider hosts that have good reviews, have had their identity verified (a little green tick appears near their photo) and in reading their profile information, it seems like we'd get along / have a lot to talk about (they don't have to be into the same things I'm into, but at least seem like they are open to learning and sharing). You can refine searches to stay with couples, only women or men. There are such a diverse range of hosts!

I've found it to be always a fabulous learning and sharing experience. I've made good friends. I've also made good friends by attending Couchsurfing events in various cities I've been in. So even if I'm not Couchsurfing with a host, I attend events (events are open to everyone and there are weekly meet-ups in almost every city and often a huge range of activities are held by various Couchsurfing members). You can also go onto the Couchsurfing forum for the city and see if anyone else wants to do an activity you want to do, or you can join with someone else to explore a place.

My summary and tips on Couchsurfing:

- ✔ Definitely get a Couchsurfing (CS) profile happening before you travel.

- ✔ If you have time, attend a CS event in your own city before you leave (making connections on your profile is helpful).

- ✔ Thoroughly check out hosts before you decide to stay: read their profile (it is about connecting and learning from people who you think will be interesting to spend time with - it's not just about a free bed!); check their reviews from other surfers; make sure they are verified!

- ✔ Use the Couchsurfing site to connect with other like-minded travelers whilst you're in town.

- ✔ Attend local CS events.

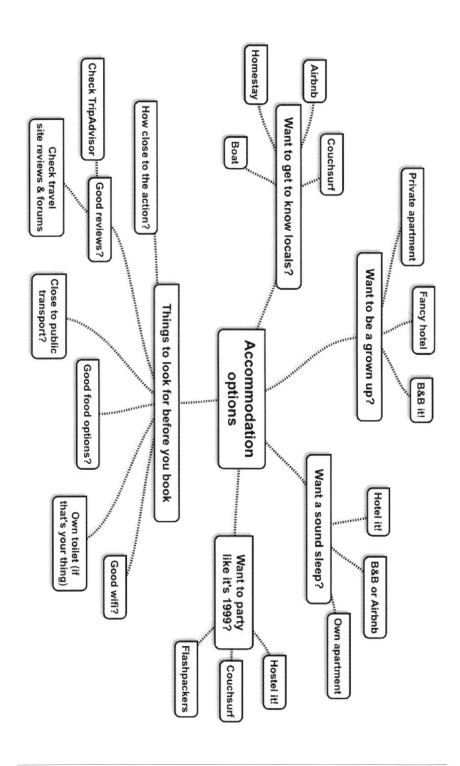

5. When you're there (i.e. get out)

It may seem obvious, but the best way to enjoy all a place has to offer is to get out of your accommodation.

I know some travelers who have been to a new place, checked into their hotel, gone out to dinner or just drinks, spent the night at a bar, then left the next day. According to them, they have 'seen' the place. They have certainly seen a town through its drinking establishment/s, and that may be enough for them. That is ok, but I'm here to tell you there is a whole big wide world out there for you to explore and enjoy in each and every town you visit.

In the same place I met the travelers who drank and left the next day, I explored for a couple of days, wandering the streets framed with 18th Century buildings, tripped over cobble stones, found hidden away cafes, met a local artist and learnt about a local secret society. Certainly you may meet some interesting locals (or foreigners) drinking one night at a bar which you may or may not remember the next day. It's a different experience than my friends, but one I have found to be a very full and rich.

This chapter overviews some of the ways you can find out activities for a place, food, free walking tours and what to take out with you (during the day and at night).

Activities

There are such a range of activities in each location you visit and these vary depending on the natural environment, historical drawcards, local specialties, the season and the local enterprises that have sprung up around the town and tourists. What you're interested in determines the path you take.

I have rocked cooking classes in Oaxaca; loved elephants in Chiang Mai, hired out a dodgem-esque vehicle to explore mountainous countryside in Ecuador, sweated Samba lessons in Rio, flew a light plane over the Nazca lines in Peru, fell off my pushbike into a river in Vietnam, walked alone in the mountains of Northern India, learnt Espanol for 5 weeks in Buenos Aires… the list continues!

Wherever you stay, there is usually a lot of advertising material about the things to do in town. If not, there are plenty of other ways of finding out your local options. These are:

- **Information centers.** I love tourist information centers! Usually they have the most up to date information on activities and tours in your location. A word of caution though: make sure you find the 'official' tourist office if you can. Many tour booking agencies have signs out the front 'tourist information' (or something similar) and in essence they are there to sell activities where they can make commission. There might be more or better options out there, so seek out the town's official tourist information center.

Occasionally, some official information centers only promote tours that they get some benefit from as well. The best way I know to confirm the quality of an activity is to check TripAdvisor for reviews.

- **TripAdvisor.** Search top things to do in each locale.

- **Search** on your favorite search engine 'top things to do in …(town)'. You will inevitably get reviews, a few blogs, travel magazine entries & local travel companies.

- **Lonely Planet online.** Gone are the days when the majority of people carry around their heavy 'Lonely Planet' guides for each country. It's now all online & at your fingertips. There are some free as well as paid information on Lonely Planet's website.

- **Ask people** (other tourists and locals) in your accommodation or at cafes what are their favorite things to do in town. I've found sometimes the best tips come from this.

- **Ask on a couchsurfing.com forum.** Often there are great local tips of what to do around town from locals.

Travel insurance note:

When you decide which activity you want to do, check your travel insurance to see if it is covered. If it isn't, you will have to make the choice about whether you want to continue the activity. Most of the time it is fine of course, but there is always that one occasion.

Free walking tours

I remember my very first free walking tour in Paris. An animated guide with the most interesting stories woven into the theme of the tour. I ended up going on 6 different walking tours throughout Paris that week! All the guides were smart, knew a lot about the history of Paris and were great storytellers.

It was from then on I sought out free walking tours in every city I went to. Free walking tours continue to mushroom up all over the world. The concept has caught on. It's a way for students (and others) to support themselves through University (or otherwise) and the perfect way to get an initial, excellent glimpse into the history and various lives surrounding the city.

Tip: Even though it is a free walking tour, you are encouraged to leave a tip for the guide (they are not paid in any other form). Please tip generously, usually the walk and talk is for 3 or more hours in the rain or sunshine and they put in a lot of effort. If you were booking a private tour, it would cost you much more than what you will give this guide. It's a good deal all round.

Eating

I adore food. Thoroughly and completely. And I have dietary requirements. This has led me on paths of marvelous adventure in new towns and cities across the world. It has caused me to research and find hidden away places, local hangouts, where rarely a tourist ventures.

My first big tip for eating is to ask a local what is their favorite food hangout. Eating at local places allows you to sample local delights and watch people (another of my cherished hobbies). Often you will get better tips doing this than two hours of solid internet research.

If you have dietary requirements, then you will need to do a bit more investigation. My hands down go-to-love website (it has saved me all over the world) is:

www.happycow.net

What is great about this site is it has health food stores as well as restaurants (you can search for gluten free places for example). It has vegetarian and vegan restaurants listed for even the most random place, and importantly restaurants that are veg friendly (so if you are traveling with both meat eaters and veg only eaters everyone will be happy!). It is free and peer reviewed, which is incredibly handy to find out whether hunting down the place is worth it.

Of course there is TripAdvisor and firing up your choice search engine might get you some other results. Some cities have helpful websites which contain tourism activities and recommendations for restaurants for particular cuisines etc.

Most of all enjoy! I love sampling new cuisines, flavors and tastes. It is really the one thing I look forward to the most when I travel to a new place.

Staying longer & making new friends

If you happen to be staying in town for a bit longer, there are a few great ways to meet locals or other travelers and do fun activities together:

- couchsurfing.com. Make sure you develop a profile before you go with the tips I've outlined in the chapter 'Beds & where to sleep'. This is a great site where you can find out if there are people going on trips or you can ask whether anyone wants to do a particular activity with you or hang out.

- meetup.com. A fabulous site I've used all over the world. There are meetup groups based around all sorts of different activities in most large cities across the globe. There are social groups, specific interest groups, sports groups, business groups, you name it, there is a social group for it. I've always met a wide variety of people and ages through the meetup groups.

- internations.org. This is a social group aimed at professional ex-pats. They hold social group meetings and various other activities.

- FB groups. There are usually a few FB groups for locals and ex-pats living in the location you want to visit. Some are targeted just for people living there, and others can be more social.

- The tinder app. This is a dating app. If you are interested in potentially making friends or something else, this app can be for you. Make sure you state upfront you're only in town for a short while and whether or not you are interested in just friendships or other possibilities.

Before you leave your accommodation

A personal note: I am water obsessed. In fact, I have so much of a love affair with water that I take it wherever I go: to bed, upstairs, downstairs, walks, shops, movies, in the car. I do not leave a room without my trusty water bottle, let alone a country. I love it. I do.

Whilst some of the below list may seem OTT to most, once you have your pack sorted for the country and climate you're in, you don't have to think about it again. I always have my travel insurance details saved in my phone and know the emergency numbers, so I don't think about it after that. I have a little pack in my bag that has most of the 'essentials' like hand gel, so I don't need to think about that either. You're free to completely enjoy.

That brings me to another important point: your small front-pack / carry on. Always carry a proper small backpack that you can carry over both your shoulders! You don't want neck pains throughout your holidays because you're carrying a bag a funny way for your spine. I always have a small, light over the shoulder bag for going out in the evenings where I don't take even a sixth of the stuff listed below (the lighter, the better drinking night I say!).

I've been in travel groups where people have said, 'Why are you carrying that bag?' and then they ask me for the mosquito repellant later on that day. That's why. Being prepared means being a happy traveler. Believe me. I'd rather have the repellant and a seemingly big everyday bag than the itchy bites all night, wouldn't you?

So before you go out for the day, here is a handy list to check off.

Day Pack Checklist

- ✔ Hat
- ✔ Sunscreen
- ✔ Water bottle
- ✔ Snacks (I've regularly gotten stuck somewhere or been absorbed in an activity and having a packet of nuts has saved me on many occasion).
- ✔ Map of town or locale (& addresses of places you intend to visit).
- ✔ Accommodation card (incl. address and phone number - it's super easy then to hand over to a taxi driver if you get lost!).
- ✔ Phone number of your travel insurance & policy number.
- ✔ Local emergency numbers.
- ✔ Money. I usually take as much money as I think I will need for the day and then extra (for just in case). I only take my ATM card with me when I need to withdraw cash.
- ✔ Wallet & copy of ID / Passport (many countries require you to carry a copy of your passport with you at all times

- I've never been asked, but handy to have and some activities have required my passport details - easy to hand over if you always carry a copy). If I am hiring out a car, I'll take my driver's license with me.

✔ Camera (fully charged).

✔ Phone (useful for making local calls or connecting to Wi-Fi if available).

✔ Spork (you can eat just about anything with this light, easy to pack and fit in anywhere item).

✔ Swiss army knife (amazing how useful it is).

✔ Small torchlight (or light attached to phone).

✔ Sensible walking shoes (it is SO worth looking boring in comfortable shoes - although there are a lot of cool traveling shoes out there these days - to be able to walk around for long periods of time without getting sore feet). Your feet and legs will thank you, believe me.

✔ Hand gel / wipes.

✔ Tissues (unbelievably useful for those emergency toilet stops).

✔ Deodorant (yes I hate body odor smell & avoid it at all costs).

✔ Facial wipes (a god send on a hot day especially). I also carry a reusable face wipe (from a travel shop) for those ultra-hot and humid climates.

✔ Breath mints (well, you never know).

✔ Band-Aids and antiseptic gel.

✔ Mosquito repellant (at dusk, wherever you are, it's so worth not getting bitten).

✔ Rain shower cover for my front-pack (I love my camera & my computer - so this is essential in my book).

If your activities involve water, add in:

✔ Towel

✔ Bathers

✔ Flip-flops

✔ Potential changes of clothes / underwear

✔ Water proof pack for your camera / wallet

✔ Tampons

At night

Going out at night means you get to see a different side to a place you are exploring. I enjoy seeing how a place lights up (or otherwise!) in the evenings. See my chapters 'Going out, drinking and drugs' and 'Safety' for more tips and advice on going out at night.

Generally, I take as little as possible out at night. If I am just going out for dinner and then heading home and I want to do some work whilst I am out, then I will carry my small backpack with my computer (but empty the day stuff out). As a general rule, I don't take my big camera out at night. Occasionally I do if I know the place and area and feel pretty comfortable wandering around with my big camera by myself.

What I usually take out most nights is a light, small shoulder bag, and I always put an emergency note in my bra (the amount of a taxi ride home). I never take a credit card or ATM card out at night (unless I am exceptionally familiar and comfortable with a place - I withdraw money ahead of time and keep any cards back at my accommodation).

I have the details of restaurants, bars and photos of maps saved in my phone so that I can refer to them when I need to. Saves space (and paper!).

Night bag

- ✔ Tissues
- ✔ Hand gel
- ✔ Lip Balm
- ✔ Small purse with just the amount I want to spend that evening
- ✔ Photocopy of ID
- ✔ The accommodation details of where I'm staying
- ✔ My mobile phone (including emergency contact & travel insurance dets)

6. Traveling once you're there

There are usually many options to move about a town and country when you arrive. This chapter contains tips and hints on how to get the most out of your transport experiences in a place.

Have a look at the chapter 'When you're there' for tips on what to take for day trips and at night. This chapter is all about transport.

I am a massive fan of public transport. Not only is it better for the environment, as a cultural seeker, you can learn a lot about local people by catching local transport. It can be uncomfortable, smelly and in your face, but it can also lead to great interactions between you and the residents.

Doing it like a local: transport around the town

Before you leave your accommodation

Even if you speak the language fluently, navigating the local public transport system can be complicated. If possible, ask a resident or any locals at your accommodation about:

- The exact place to catch / get on transport (I've been to many places where transport signs do not exist - I like a place that keeps you guessing)
- The particular platforms

- The approximate fares (try and carry the correct change because more often than not, drivers cannot change big notes)

- Whether you need to use machines to use the transport (and how they operate)

- If you don't speak the language, get them to write down the name of the spot or places you want to go to (and then write down for you the phonetics of the word(s) so that you can ask someone as well - many people all over the world have not learnt to read).

- The other best option is getting a map of the transport system (or downloading it onto your phone. There are surprisingly many apps available, especially for the larger cities you visit). That way you can follow the stops along the route.

Buses

Buses vary dramatically in comfort and quality in countries across the globe. In some places you are guaranteed a seat in air-conditioned opulence, in others you will be sharing a two seat space with 5 people (and your day pack and whatever they are carrying) and you wonder if you will ever breathe again. Some will have windows and in some, you will feel the fresh blast of dusty air on your face as you meander through unpaved streets, dodging carts, non human animals, children and veggie stands.

Trains

I thoroughly enjoy train travel. Day train travel in particular. Some overnight trains in Asia leave a lot to be desired, but in a few hours, you can experience and learn so much about local life.

I caught a local train from Mangalore to Goa in India. When I first got on, I had a whole seat to myself. Within a few stops, I was knees up over my backpack jammed against the window. The first group of people to sit beside me was a Hindu family which included two sisters, one with a husband and about 5 children between them. Most of the journey, one sister and three or four children shared the seat with me.

"Hello, what is your name?"

"My name is Susmita. What is yours?"

"Sunni, like a sunny day."

"That is like Indian name, but for men, but you are a girl."

"Yes I am."

"Where are you from? … Would you like some of these?…"

I was hounded with questions and offerings of food they bought with them or purchased from the many men and women shuffling and heaving heavy baskets through the cramped isle.

The crunch of salty and sweet filled my mouth over and over again.

"This is my boy, he is very naughty"

I smiled, "Why is he naughty?"

"He never does what he's told, very disobedient. And too much energy."

"He looks very lively to me."

"He needs to go to boarding school in Australia. There, he will be taught rules. You can adopt him."

I smiled, "Really?"

"Yes, really, he needs discipline. Take him to Australia."

"I don't think I'm ready to raise a child yet."

"You will be good. Australia will be good."

"Okay."

I knew she was serious. I couldn't quite believe that I had only met her 40 minutes ago and she was more than willing to give me her child. I could have been a mother immediately. It was a strange feeling.

When the family got off the train, they all waited, grouped together and waved until the train motioned forward once again. *Wow.*

The next large family to join me was comprised completely of veiled women and one man. I smiled and said 'hello' as a few of them with children sat beside me. The man that was with them was forced to sit a few seats ahead with some more veils and children.

The woman beside me spoke eagerly to me in a thick accent. She wanted to know everything about me. Was I married? Why am I traveling alone? Do I have photos of Australia? I really wished at that moment that I did keep some photos on my phone of Australia to show her - she particularly wanted to see photos of my family and friends.

We talked for a long period of time. The man that was with her kept motioning for her to come sit in a seat ahead of him. She continuously refused and kept the conversation going with me. She explained she was an English teacher in her village and had never traveled outside her area. She was so eager for information from the outside world.

Towards the end of our time together, she showed me photos of her without her veil. She had long, beautiful curly hair and deep brown eyes. It was initially hard for me to marry this voice, her heavily stilted English with this picture, her eyes alight with joy and laughter. When she told me she had to leave, she asked me for a hug.

I gave her a big hug. I was so touched.

The magic of catching a 6-hour local train in India. The hard metal seats, no windows, and being cramped up over my backpack against the side. It was perhaps my most enjoyable train ride, ever. I learnt so much in those 6 hours and connected with people I wouldn't ordinarily have had a chance to meet.

Trams

I love cities that use trams. Trams give a city a unique feel. They are a great way to glide along and see a city. If there is a city with a tram, I highly recommend using them. They never disappoint. Ever. Some of the cities I've ridden in delight with this form of travel: Melbourne, Casablanca, San Francisco, Bordeaux, New Orleans, and Istanbul.

Boat / Ferry

Another favorite of mine (yes, I have too many favorites) is boat and ferry travel. Seeing a place through its waterways, lakes or oceans is a unique and usually incredibly beautiful way to enjoy a city. Sydney of course is one that springs to mind as a place that does this so incredibly well, and who can pass up Venice? Istanbul has another marvelous ferry adventure and a great way to cross between the two divides of Asia and Europe.

I would encourage everyone to use local transport as much as possible. It gives you different insights into a city. You never know who you may meet and what you may see or find!

Local transport to travel to your next destination

You may also want to use local transport to travel to the next destination within a country. This can be a great option. Many well set up tourist places will have 'tourist' buses that will take you to the next popular tourist destination. Often when you are in popular tourist spots, it is the only option you are given. So while it's local, it's separated from the most local form of transport.

The tourist buses I've taken in Asia and South America have been great and usually very cheap. I do recommend the tourist bus option for travel between cities. I actually feel a bit safer traveling as a single woman surrounded by other tourists, especially in overnight buses.

Of course in many locations, you will only have local bus or train options. I now have flashbacks to buses stopping in random locations in the middle of the night, forcing you out of buses into large fluorescently lit centers of inedible food and strong smelling toilets that you really don't want to use your torchlight in. Really, you don't.

These sleep disturbed nights, funky excretion holes and long hours of whizzing dark sights are all a part of the travel experience. Some you would prefer not to engage with, but it is a part of the adventure and you can enjoy a hot shower and a good bed at the end of the trip. The simple stuff I enjoy to a far greater extent. I love that.

My tips for traveling to your next destination

Generally, you will need to buy a ticket in advance to reserve your seat. When you do that, it's great if you can get the following details at the same time (pretty similar to the above checklist):

- The exact place to catch / get on transport

- The particular platforms / bus bays

- The approximate fares (try and carry the correct change always)

- Whether you need to use ticket machines to use the transport (and how they operate)

- If you don't speak the language, get them to write down the name of the place you want to go to (and then write down for you the phonetics of the word/s so that you can ask someone as well - many people all over the world have not learnt to read).

- Know whether your stop is the last stop. If it is, you won't miss it! If it's not, ask the driver to tell you when to get off. I also try and find out approximately how long the journey is supposed to take, so around that time I am alert, start looking more closely out the window and I'm ready to go.

Handy tip

If you are traveling to a small town or village, find out before you go whether the town has ATMs. Not all places will have an ATM, and having money to continue on, is kinda handy.

Do an internet search on town facilities and talk to people who have recently been there (which is usually the most helpful as they will have the most up to date information).

Take enough cash with you that you think will get you through to the next major city (you don't want to carry too much cash in case anything happens).

Local Transport Checklist

Try to find out:

✔ The exact place to catch / get on transport (I've been to many places where transport signs do not exist - I like a place that keeps you guessing).

✔ The particular platforms.

✔ The approximate fares (try and carry the correct change -more often than not drivers cannot change big notes).

✔ Whether you need to use machines to use the transport (and how they operate);

✔ If you don't speak the language, get them to write down the name of the spot or places you want to go to (and then write down for you the phonetics of the word/s so that you can ask someone as well - many people all over the world have not learnt to read).

✔ Know whether your stop is the last stop.

✔ The other best option is getting a map of the transport system (or downloading it on your phone - there are surprisingly many apps available, especially for the larger cities you visit). This way, you can follow the stops along the route.

7. Going out, drinking & drugs

Checking out local bars

I have regularly gone out to local bars by myself across the globe. As a single woman, it can be a bit daunting. Being alone for a start. Then, more importantly, there are safety considerations. So when I do go out, I plan ahead. I have a map of the area with me, my accommodation details, I know how the taxis work (and how safe they are) and I learn a bit about where I'm heading out to. I recommend reading this chapter alongside my specific safety tips outlined in the chapter 'Safety'.

A couple of tales from my nocturnal experiences:

Grand Granada

Granada in Southern Spain captivated me from the moment I arrived. It's medieval churches and cobble stones greeted me. I strolled around the cute squares of green and gushed every day over the foreboding beauty crowning the town: the Alhambra. A magical jewel in Islamic architecture in which the very Catholic conquering Queen Ann insisted on being buried. I would too!

I wanted to check out the nightlife and see if it could beguile me as much as the town. I found a bar that seemed my kinda scene. It was a Saturday night. Fun night. I sat by myself and ordered a 'Vino Tinto.'

I looked around at the tables next to me: tables of men guzzling their cool liquids, some bopping to the music. Some distance away, I noticed a table of very funky looking women. Animated, cool haircuts and sharp clothes.

I decided to move a little closer to hear their conversation. Not to pry into their business, but to hear if they were speaking Spanish or English.

Damn, they are speaking Spanish. What a shame. I wish I knew a lot more Spanish! *Hang on, they are speaking some English now. Interesting.*

I ordered another Vino Tinto.

I continued to observe them. They seemed so cool. I really wanted to know them. But I didn't want to be the imposing English speaking foreigner.

I ordered another. *What the heck, it's now or never.*

I took my glass over to them and said, "Hello." They seemed a little taken aback and passed odd looks to each other.

"I'm Sunni and I'm from Australia. I'm visiting here. I totally love this city."

Their faces turned into somewhat smiles, this crazy intruder. *Luckily, I'm from the other side of the world.*

I started to make conversation with one woman. They all could speak perfect English and Spanish. *Well jell*, as they say in Essex! *Oh to be bilingual!*

As I involved one of them in conversation, the others relaxed. More funksters joined us and I was introduced. Then I became included in rounds of drinks. That was it. I was in!

I ended up spending the entire evening with these fabulous women, drinking, dancing and a few of them invited me back to their place. I went. We drank until the light came. They even invited me to stay with them. And I would have if I hadn't booked my travel already for the next day.

It was a great experience. After summoning up the courage to talk to these women, I ended up having a fabulous evening and making new friends which I keep in touch with to this day.

For some more inspiration, I'll tell you a story of when I encouraged a young woman who was a bit sad and feeling sorry for herself to go out and explore on her own.

Lonely Lisbon?

I was staying in a very funky accommodation spot in Lisbon and I met two girls. They had both been out during the day and watched a fabulous jazz concert in the park. They were approached by a young man who dazzled one of them in particular and invited her out to dinner that evening. Her fellow female traveling companion pretended to be happy for her, but really she was very jealous and upset with her friend for leaving her alone for the evening. That's when I met her.

"She's just gorgeous with her big black curly hair and sharp looks, guys are always fawning all over her!"

"Lucky her."

"Yer, but we are traveling together, and I thought that she would say no, so that I wouldn't have to spend a night alone. I'm a bit angry at her really."

I nodded. "Yes, it's hard sometimes when you expect certain things from your friends."

"Of course, we are traveling together. We are supposed to be best friends. What am I supposed to do tonight then?"

"You could go out by yourself."

"No way. I'd look like a loser."

"Well, I've traveled a lot by myself now and I LOVE going out by myself. I've met loads of interesting people and had loads of great experiences."

"Really?"

"Yes, absolutely."

"And I won't look like a loser?"

"Not at all. You're traveling, it's okay to be by yourself."

"I don't know."

"I absolutely promise you, that if you do it, you won't be disappointed. I know it will work out for you."

"Really, but how do I talk to people?"

"You are a beautiful, smart woman, and you can easily make conversations with people. It all starts with 'Hello'."

She smiles, I continue. "Then you won't be so angry at your friend. You will be doing something for yourself. Try it out. Just see. I would go out with you, but I'm exhausted tonight and I need sleep. But I know you can do it."

I talked to her for about an hour and a half. Going over the same fears and anger. But by the end she was all nervous and excited about the possibility.

…

The following day, I met her bounding around the kitchen.

"Oh my god, I took your advice and went out. You won't believe what happened!"

"I can't wait."

She was all smiles and bubbles, "Well, I went to this bar and started talking to the barman. He was cute. We kept talking all evening between him serving drinks. I spoke to some other people at the bar too. The guy owned the bar, so he said he could take me back here, and he came back here with me!!!"

"Oh wow - *here??*"

"Yup. I knew Francesca wouldn't be here. So we had some time together and then he had to go close the bar and come back. I agreed that I would come down and let him in in an hour because I don't have a Portuguese Sim card. I was waiting for him and then I must have fallen asleep because I didn't wake up until Francesca came back!"

"OMG, he must have been waiting for you downstairs."

"Yes, poor guy."

"Was it good sex?"

"Yes, it was fun, I mean, we were a bit tired, but it was good. He was hot!"

"Great to hear!"

"And it's all because of you! I am so glad I took your advice and went out!"

"I'm so happy for you! Yah!"

Doing it yourself

It is more than possible for you too to go out and make new friends when you're in another country. Sometimes, I've made great friends that I've hung out with for the rest of the weekend, other times I've just had really fun conversations and gone home early. Sometimes I've had one drink and gone home. More often than not, when I have gone out, I've had a great time. Here are my tips for doing it alone as a solo woman:

- Know the area (the bar area generally and where you're going). I take a small fold up map with me if I can or take a photo on my phone of the map of the area from my computer. It works totally fine. (Most of the time I haven't had a sim card and data pack in the various countries I've visited and instead just had Wi-Fi when I've been at my accommodation and/ or cafes. So I prep ahead by taking photos of where I'm going so I know what to look for! It's good practice regardless of whether you do have data, just in case the network is down).

- Have a card or photo of the card of your accommodation and phone numbers (I usually let the accommodation people know I'm going out, the general area I'm heading out to and check in with them about the safety of the area and taking taxis from the area).

- Have the details of your travel insurance in your phone.
- Have local police numbers and emergency numbers in your phone contacts too.
- When you arrive, try and see where you can take a taxi home (look for the taxi ranks etc.). I find it reassuring knowing that I can confidently walk in the direction of the taxi rank when I leave a bar.

When I'm prepared, then I relax. Of course the first glass of *vino tinto* helps me get into the mood too!

How to get over any potential fears of walking into a bar, alone:

- Tell yourself that it's okay that you don't have any friends here. You are new here. This is perfectly reasonable and an opportunity to make new friends.
- Men go out all the time alone, sit at a bar and drink. If it's normal and okay for men to do it, it's okay for you too.
- Give yourself an out. Tell yourself if you don't feel comfortable, you can either move onto another place or go home. No loss.
- Bring a smartphone to play with. It's a good initial distraction (I find when I'm focusing on something else initially, I relax and get more comfortable in a space).
- Once you've had the first drink (or two), start to look around more. If there are people you think look interesting, smile. Say hello if you feel game. I find as soon

as I say hello, that's it. A conversation begins and then your whole inner world changes. You've done it, and if this conversation doesn't work out, the next one will. It's way easier the second time!

Drugs

Don't do drugs. But if you do, investigate a few things first.

What to be aware of

Buying drugs off the street in any random city (I am continuously astounded about how many times I've been offered drugs in various cities around the world), you need to seriously remember the following:

- You don't know the quality of the drug or if the drug is safe to take.
- You don't know the person you are buying from.
- You don't know if that person is a police officer (and you could be caught with charges).
- You don't know if it will end in bribes (and do you have enough cash to get out of it and are you sure that will be enough or that that will be the end of it??).
- You don't know if you will be followed (another safety risk).

Know the law!

Also, very importantly, know the local laws! Generally knowing the drug laws in a country will help you determine if you take the risk. For example, being caught with 20 grams of ecstasy in Thailand carries a death sentence. In the Netherlands, the prison sentence for personal use of ecstasy ranges between 1 week and 2 months. Just slightly different penalties!

Smoking marijuana for personal use in the Netherlands will evoke police dismissal and possession of up to 1kg will result in a fine. In Thailand if you test positive to consuming marijuana, it's one year in prison and if you are carrying any on you, it can be up to 5 years imprisonment. Again, just slightly different penalties. The penalties are vastly harsher if they believe that you are dealing or smuggling and carry death penalty sentences in Thailand. Knowing the law really helps you to assess whether you take a risk in a particular country. And most importantly consider again the above dot points (I'm not a nerd really, just practical :)).

8. Romantic liaisons

Oh the travel love affair! You've heard of them. You've seen them on the movies. Is it real? Does it work? The answer is both yes and no. There are a few things to be aware of in the sought after / idealized holiday romance. I've had a few romances on the road. And they have been super fun at times, heart wrenching at others, confusing and hilarious in many other moments. I'm currently writing about some of these in my upcoming book 'The secret diaries of a solo woman traveler'. You'll have to read it to get all the down and dirty juicy stories. But for the purposes of this book, I'll keep it to the basics about what you need to think about if you decide to venture into this terrain.

Here's what I've learnt

- **Be upfront.** This is for you as much as them. You are only there for a short period of time. Let them know this. You just aren't in any position to make any promises.

- **Romantic visions are just that.** Visions. You can be taken up in the moments of fun loving freedom you are experiencing at the time. Life is different when you're on holidays. So is love. Just be mindful that you are in a different space that is full of adventure, you are not in your usual life or routine. When routine happens, away or at home, life and love changes. You are different. So are they. So enjoy it now.

- **Don't fall in love!** Just re-iterating the above in stronger terms. Long distance relationships rarely work. Especially new relationships. Keep this bit of priceless knowledge in the back of your head.

- **Test the waters.** Maybe they are the guy or girl who likes to play around with the fresh new blood in town. This might or might not be okay with you. It might be okay because you are just there for a fleeting time. It might not be okay because you're not generally into those sorts of people. You'll have to work that one out for yourself.

One way to work out if you want to hang out with a person any longer is to meet them the following day. Often a first meeting with someone is fun and exciting. You have a drink, maybe food, they are excited and perhaps you are too. The next meeting tells me more about the type of person they are.

Questions to potentially ask yourself are:

- do we have as much to talk about today?
- do they annoy me?
- do we have things in common?
- is there a buzzy feeling? (you know the one, the one that excites and arouses you, that you are jittery about what might happen next...).

Cultural dynamics

You may be that person who finds a lover that lives down the road from you in your home town that you just never met. Cross cultural dynamics and miscommunications are likely to be a lot less if this is the case. For everyone else traveling overseas, if you meet and fall in love with other travelers or a local, you are likely to experience the complete joy of cross cultural communication. And it is a joy. But can be completely confusing at the same time.

Some of what you are likely to experience:

Language barriers.

If you meet someone whose language is not the first language you also spoke at home, there are likely to be some communication issues. It can be very fun indeed to not understand what someone has said, but it can also be frustrating when you can't communicate what you want to. I have had some hugely frustrating times when I say something and know that it has not been understood. I often check with the person:

"What do you think I just said?"

This question alone tells me how little or how much they have understood what I just told them. When I am with someone whose second, third or fourth language is English, I always take the time to speak and enunciate my words clearly. I try to do this effortlessly (so that the other person doesn't know that I'm intentionally being slow). I get the following comment from people everywhere:

"I understand you, but I don't understand other Australians or English people."

It really doesn't take much to be a bit more thoughtful in how you speak. And it works wonders for your relationships.

Misunderstandings of body language.

There are many examples of where body language means different things in different countries. My favorite example is the Indian head sway. The 'head sway' is literally just that. It is a slight movement of the head from left to right or right to left, sometimes multiple times. I asked my Indian friend," What does the head sway mean, yes or no?"

"It means 'Yes', 'No', or 'Maybe."

"All three?"

"Yes."

"That makes it difficult to understand what people mean then."

"Yes, well you have to look for other clues as to understand what they are meaning."

"Right."

I recently spoke to a Nepali professor on this very subject and she told me that why western people generally have a problem with the head sway is that in the West, we want definite answers. We are obsessed with knowing exactly what is meant, rather than being happy with any in between. I find that interesting.

Not understanding what love means in different contexts.

Love means things in different contexts. In some countries, being interested in someone is tantamount to an engagement, with a wedding in close future proximity. This can be overwhelming to a modern western woman who wouldn't consider an engagement until months or years after knowing someone very well indeed. These are hard and murky waters to navigate. I have had many a man wanting to marry me soon after we have started seeing each other.

Different expectations of roles of men and women.

This may or may not be as obvious in same sex relationships, but in heterosexual relationships, the roles of women and men can vary greatly between countries. For me personally, I have found that hard to envisage for myself in different countries where the men expect to be looked after in all home activities, regardless of whether the woman works outside the home all day. This is a big issue for me.

Different understandings of time.

This is an extremely common cultural clash, not just in relationships between minority world ('western') countries and majority world ('developing') countries.

Recently I had a conversation with a guy in Morocco.

"Time is not important to us. If we make an appointment to meet in a coffee shop and you show up 2 hours late, no problem, I will wait for you."

Coming from a society where being on time is very important and where it is considered rude if you do not show up on time, I have struggled with this on many occasions (this is common in many cultures right across the globe). I've learnt to relax a little and as long as I have a book or computer to occupy myself, I can go with the flow a bit more. But, the truth is, it is a sticking point that I haven't yet fully embraced. But maybe it'll work for you!

The passport thing.

One final matter to be aware of is the passport thing. If you happen to be from Europe, the UK, North America, Australia or New Zealand, then there may be a possibility that the guy or girl you meet is interested in your passport. It's worth being upfront and questioning motivations at the start of the romance (without trying to be too skeptical - it's a fine balance). You may be fine with them being interested in both you and the passport, it's just good to be aware of.

If you are just interested in sex, that is great!

You might know that you are simply interested in having sex. An empowered woman who is happy to have her physical needs met is simply wonderful. Sometimes it's just nice to have your body adored for an evening, morning or long afternoon. ;)

Always carry condoms (and/or dams, gloves, depending on your thing).

I always carry condoms. I have quite a few in my main toiletry bag, but I also carry two condoms (hidden away in a secret corner) of my smaller day pack (I've rarely needed or used them, but they are terribly handy to have on that odd occasion you need them. Or if a friend does!). I am truly the ultimate preparer.

Meet the following day!

I was in New Orleans doing what I love to do best: wandering the streets with my camera in hand. It was nearing the end of magic hour and I was taking my last photos of Jackson Square. I noticed a very attractive gentleman watching me. I smiled.

He smiled back, approaching me. "You're taking a photo of the square?" *Really? Could it be any more obvious?*

"Yes, it's a perfect time of day to take photos." I moved to away from him to take a picture from a slightly different angle (*because that makes all the difference of course*).

"Where are you from?"

"Guess."

"England." *I wish that someone guessed Swaziland one day - why just the obvious boring options?*

"No."

"Well, I don't think you're from Canada. Somewhere in Europe?"

"No."

"Australia."

"Well done. At least you mentioned it, most Americans never guess Australia. I guess it's just so far away!"

"Is photography one of your hobbies? It looks like you enjoy taking a lot of pictures."

"Yes I do and yes it is. I'm going to continue now, nice to meet you."

"Can I walk with you a bit, are you going to continue taking pictures?"

"Yes I am. And I need to eat. I am desperate for some fried green tomatoes."

"I know just the place."

"Great."

It wasn't just his beauty that engaged me. He kept me entertained with politics and family law. Everyone wants to tell me their story when they know I've practiced family law, and I'm okay with that, it tells me a lot about a person on how they handled their divorce.

After some fried green tomatoes he took me to some live music in the best street of New Orleans. It was a Monday night, but the tunes were pumping.

After a few drinks we started getting closer to each other. He was exactly my type physically, and although he had a few hang ups about the divorce, he was smart. I like smart. So I could see myself having a fling with him, I was just exhausted and really needed to go home.

His big lips felt perfect on mine and I liked holding his large hands.

"I'm really very tired and I do need to go home."

"Let's go for a walk."

"Ok."

"I want to stay with you tonight."

"I know, I'm just very tired. I'm happy to meet up tomorrow."

"We could just sleep together. We don't need to do anything."

"You and I both know that that would be impossible."

"Can I come back with you?"

"No, look I need to know you a bit better before we do this."

"You're welcome to come back with me."

"No, I don't feel comfortable with that tonight. I need to know you a little more."

"Can we meet up tomorrow then, I have some time."

"Sure thing. Here's my number."

The next day I kept checking my phone. Nothing. I was almost certain he would call. And he knew I was leaving the next day.

Late afternoon and evening came. Nothing. *I thought that he was really into me. Oh well, it's not like I wanted any more from him than another fun evening, and he was so my type.*

He never ended up calling. Of course a whole range of things could have happened to make him not contact me, but he didn't even text to say that. *That is so not my type.*

Why am I sharing this story? The best advice I was given from a fellow woman traveler was to ask to meet them the next day. Then you know if they are really keen, and you find out whether you want to spend 5 minutes more with each other or it was just a drunken whim from the night before. Also, the buildup I find can be quite stirring.

Of course drunken whims can be perfectly great too, it just depends what you prefer, or what you're into. Enjoy!

9. Debriefing and looking after you

One of the things I believe is undervalued and under thought of when traveling is being able to talk to someone about your experiences, the travel itself and other things from home that you're thinking about. Let's face it, there will always be something (work, home, hobbies), or some people (relationships, former lovers, family members, friends) you will be contemplating or processing whilst you are traveling. We don't set out with a clean slate or have the ability to wipe everything away in an instant that you sip that first cocktail in the departure lounge. You wish that was the case, but the reality is rather different.

I think being aware of this before you go away is incredibly useful. Travel can often provide you with different insights and fresh perspectives with various issues and problems whilst you are away, but being prepared with tools if stuff comes up helps you feel more confident to deal with it. There are many options available to you. I've detailed these below.

The truth is, travel is sometimes very challenging and there are different degrees of challenge depending on where you are and how you are traveling. No matter where you go, travel can be at times tough with cultural misunderstandings, long delays in transport, bad food or something more dramatic. These situations can bring up your 'stuff' and having the tools to deal with it can be very useful.

When something dramatic happens whilst you are away

It is not uncommon to get a bout of stomach flu, twist an ankle or get something stolen when you travel. I hope none of this happens for you. What I have found is when a negative incident like this happens, it often brings up 'other stuff' from your life. You start thinking about the other horrible things that have happened to you, or the things in your life that you don't feel good about.

It can bring up thoughts of a past bad relationship, that your father embarrassed you when you were 11, your horrible ex-boss, the fight you had with your mother and the bad words exchanged when you were 15, your best friend falling in love with your love... you know, all things that you want to forget. They come rushing back to you in these moments.

So you need to be prepared. When you're a solo traveler, there might not be many people about that you want to talk to about your feelings or your past. Sometimes you hit it lucky and just the right person comes along whom you feel comfortable sharing your life story.

But often there isn't.

Ways to deal with it

- **Know.** Initially understanding that seemingly unassociated incidents can bring up big emotions in you. It's probably due to not completely processing / allowing yourself to feel all the stuff the first or second or third times shit happened before.

- **Cry.** I love a good crying afternoon (if I can manage to string it out for more than an hour or two!). When I allow myself to cry (and really weep if possible) I find it settles (or I settle) down after a while - sometimes after 10 minutes, 25 minutes or 95 minutes. I find completely allowing the huge emotions lets it dissipate fairly quickly. If it doesn't, that's okay too! We don't allow ourselves to cry a lot in society, usually reserved for a tear jerker at the movies, where it's socially acceptable. And only a little. I would love to see people feeling safe to cry or express emotions without monitoring it for fear of other's reactions. And people around just letting them get on with it.

What I do is create a safe space for myself (I go to my room or accommodation where no-one is around and put away my computer and phone) and cry. I always prepare with tissues and water and just let it flow as it comes. I try to really feel into my body and let the tears emerge from there.

I find that the crying often comes in waves, so I let the peaks happen and the quiet more subtle teary moments on my pillow. I stay with it. I feel like the peaks need to happen a few times so that the emotion is fully experienced. I think after a couple of rounds of this, everything that needs to come out has. I treat myself gently for the rest of the day; get a massage, take myself out to a nice meal and/or watch a movie.

- **Journal.** The most valuable tool ever! Being able to write out your feelings and let yourself write anything (without self-monitoring, focusing on correctly spelling words or thinking about anyone reading it apart from you) allows you to express sometimes that which you may not be able to formulate orally. Sometimes the mind over thinks and writing shit down changes things somehow.

- **Skype.** With a loved one. Be it a friend, co-worker, parent or sibling. There is nothing like connecting with a loved one to make you feel loved. It has been invaluable in my travels to connect with my nearest and dearest when stuff happens. It has genuinely gotten me through some pretty rough patches and made me feel that all is possible once again.

- **Set up an appointment.** You might have a regular counsellor or therapist that you could have a session online with. Or you may want to talk to an experienced travel coach who's done it all before (like me).

- **Drink.** Okay, maybe it's not the soundest advice, but hey, whatever gets you there right? (I'm mostly joking here). Having a 'night off' from your thoughts and having a good drinking and/or dancing session with new friends - preferably with a live band or board games does wonders for the spirit!

- **Treat yourself.** Take yourself out to a movie if possible or a massage or get your nails done. A bit of self-care always does wonders for the soul.

- **Watch.** Just sit and watch a sunset, wherever you are. If you can meditate or do yoga, do that. Take a moment to sit and observe what is around you.

Sometimes I do all of the above! The most important thing to know is that there are always options available to you. You are never alone in the true sense of the word and there is so much you can do to help yourself.

You can always book a flight to go back home. That is a legitimate option. And many have done so. I think a real jewel in life is being able to learn to deal with your emotions when shit happens. Travel is a perfect setup for you to do that. You are not in your usual routine. You have space and time to allow yourself to do or process things differently. Give it a try. Try doing any or all of the above suggestions and see how it works for you. The worst that can happen is you waste a few hours. The best that can happen is that you get new insights to deal with your shit or the shit the world throws at you (and you can use this again in the future).

Just check in

Sometimes, things go along fine in your travels. Great! I think it is just as important to create time out to 'check in' with you to see how it is all going.

Creating space out from your travels to journal, having time reflecting on your travels or past experiences, I think is an invaluable asset to your travel experiences. I find talking to my best friend every now and then is incredibly helpful to reflect on where I'm at and how I'm going. Often she reflects back to me how she sees me at that moment. It helps me understand if I need to spend some more time by myself (and work on my own stuff some more) or whether I'm in the flow (and that is nice feedback too).

If you don't have someone you can do that with, then you can always pay someone to help you reflect, or you can journal or think about how you are progressing in a quiet moment by yourself. The most important thing is to take time out to do this. It doesn't matter how or what or who, just that you create the time to do it.

Goals, baby, goals

I also like to think about what my goals were before I set off traveling. Was it to relax? Learn something new? How am I going with that? This is an important aspect of 'checking in' with you during your travels. It helps you then refine what you're doing.

Maybe you need to spend more time reading on the beach instead of talking endlessly with the waiters at your local restaurant, or maybe you decide that you will get out and do a historical walk around the town you are staying. Or book in to do that surfing lesson.

Or maybe you decide that learning a new skill was an overly ambitious idea and what you really need to do is just have a complete time out. That is all ok. Making a decision is what has all the power. You are deciding what is best for you at the time. This might change, and that is fine, but you are giving yourself permission to do what you need to do.

The coming and going of new friends

I have met some amazing people during my travels. People that I will stay friends with for life. Some of them I met for a day or two, others an afternoon and some I had the privilege of spending months with (when I was living down the road from them or in my volunteer work). You can develop very intense and deep friendships in a very short period of time. These are special, but it also means it can be hard to say goodbye.

Knowing about this is somewhat useful, but having some backup plans for when you may be a little sad is also good. You can try any of the above mentioned techniques. If you are traveling to a new place that's often easier because you have the excitement of a new adventure. If you are staying, it is often harder, and it's even worse if you are going home. Most people hate the end of an adventure and especially leaving people that you've connected strongly with.

It is perfectly natural to feel sad. Allow yourself to feel sad. It will make it easier to move on to your next adventure (in whatever form it takes).

Social media: I love you!

Thank the world for social media. It is an amazing tool that helps you connect with your friends and family at home, your new friends and traveling friends along the way. It is just so easy to connect and stay connected with your various networks and communities. I find social media a great tool to still feel connected with folks at home. I don't feel like I'm out of people's lives, I'm just interacting with them in different ways.

Before you leave for your travels

Before you leave for your travels, I suggest the following:

- Let people know you may want to call them while you are away. Make sure they have the same free videoing or calling tools as you (most applications require both parties to have an account with the same app): Skyping, Viber, WhatsApp, Google Hangouts, FaceTime, Facebook Messenger... there are many options. Make a few test calls to ensure it's working before you leave. There are also a number of free text and call applications you can use, that don't require both parties to have the same app. It's worth checking out.

- If you are traveling to a country where social media and/or video calling software is restricted or they have bans on the usual sites you like to use, set up a VPN account to access these sites whilst you are there (there are free and paid services. Check out hola.org for a free service). It is critical you set this up before you leave (because most of the time you won't be able to do that when you're there).

- Take a blank journal. Even a small exercise book from your local newsagent will do. Anything to allow you to express when you need to. Draw, write, and play games with yourself. You could also write your travel goals in the front of the book, so that you can reflect and journal about them as you go along.

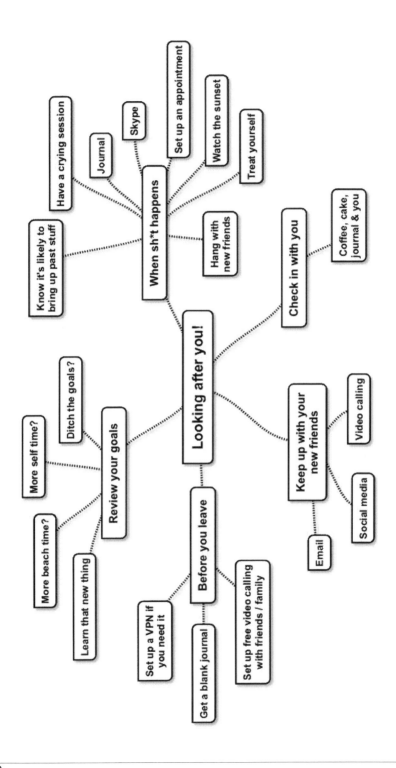

10. Safety

My main aim for this chapter is not to scare you, but to prepare you. If you are prepared, it is more likely you will be able to relax better and easier into your travels. I am always alert when I travel but I try to balance this out with a sense of relaxation when I'm walking around a new place. It's an interesting balance for sure, but one I continuously aspire to. Why? Because having a sense of ease and confidence makes you less of a target. If you feel like you have it all under control, it will show.

This has worked for me numerous times, and I'm sure it can also work for you. For example, on the day after arriving in Quito, New York, Sevilla, Istanbul and Rio, people stopped me in the streets to ask for directions. I really try to put out a 'confident, I know where I'm going' vibe wherever I walk, and it shows. Give it a try.

My sense of safety changes with the particularly country and place that I'm in. Some towns will feel a lot safer to you, others won't. One country may make you feel relaxed, and across the border you will be on hyper alert. This is the same for neighborhoods within cities. The strategies outlined in this chapter will give you good grounding for you to employ wherever you go.

Let people know where you are!

The most obvious thing to say in relation to safety (but not always done by the intrepid traveler) is to let people know where you are going and how long you'll be there. Social media makes it easier to do this. A quick check-in on FB sorts that out. Or a quick email to your loved ones back home. It doesn't need to be War and Peace, but it can be as short and simple as 'I'm here. Tired. Off to bed. Love to you all.' (that took me a whole 5 seconds to write and another 2 seconds to press 'send'. In some countries it may be a little longer depending on internet speed, but you get the idea).

Register on a government website

Most governments have a foreign office website that you can seek advice from. For example, the Australian government has a 'Smart Traveler' website which contains safety information on every country in the world and recommendations from the Australian government's perspective on safety in the country. They have different levels of caution and grading depending on the country's circumstance e.g. theft or kidnappings may be prevalent in the particular country or there may be terrorism concerns. I find it useful to read, but it hasn't yet stopped me going to a country. For example, I traveled through many countries in South America that had a 'High Level of Caution' required or recommendations not to travel and I was completely fine. I was aware that theft and kidnappings were common, but it did not stop me enjoying myself (whilst being aware of my surroundings and keeping my personal possessions close by at all times) and seeing some amazing things.

A useful tool that the Australian government has is a free register where you can register your travel destinations, plans and approximate lengths of time you are staying in a particular location. If you do not log back in within a certain period of time or an unexpected event happens, it will make it easier for the government to immediately try and find you or work on your behalf to get you out of there (or whatever the circumstance may be). So if you don't want to tell your family or friends, you could tell your government, if they have such a service.

If it's your first time in a new place

If it is your first time in a new country and you are not yet comfortable negotiating your way around new places (particularly where you don't speak the language and perhaps the place and culture is very different to your own), I would suggest it is safer and a lot more comfortable to organize a hotel / accommodation ahead of time and also a trusted transfer from the airport. In many airports and train/bus stations, you have to be careful of taxis and hawkers as they can be unsafe.

I would suggest regardless that you do a basic amount of research about taxis in the town and country you are going to before you leave. It doesn't take long to find out if taxis are safe, what sort of taxis are safe and those that are dangerous. Also whether taxis use meters or it's all by negotiation (and what the price ranges are). Taxi booking counters before you leave an airport are usually the safest. Although I have to say it is immeasurably reassuring to have a driver booked (it's often the same price as a taxi) and have the driver waiting with your name to take you to your accommodation.

If you are catching public transportation from your landing place into a new town, find out ahead of time the stop you have to get off at and directions to the accommodation from this stop.

Try to avoid arriving a night. Not only is it safer, but also you can see the area as you arrive, get the feel of the streets around your accommodation and find out the local amenities.

One of my friends Clare, who is a lover of 'free form' travel, says her strategy is when she's arriving to a new place that is a risky destination, and she is not 100% sure on the safety or otherwise of taxis or other transport, is that she looks around the plane or bus/train for other backpackers or families and sparks up conversation. She asks them where they are going and if she can share a ride with them into town. She finds it easy to make friends with other travelers, so it's a good approach if you are outgoing and it can save you money.

General recommendations

My general recommendations when traveling by yourself and walking around by yourself in a new city are:

- **Look around!** It may seem obvious, but I have gotten into a habit of looking around the street (albeit briefly) wherever I'm walking, generally observing who is around. I quickly assess the side of the street best to walk on based on the types of people, vehicles and buildings I see. It's hard to describe, but you really have to continuously trust your 'gut' on this one. I am the last person to judge someone because of their looks, but I will avoid someone if they don't have a good 'vibe'. I know that sounds vague and a bit kooky, but it's the best way I can describe it.

- **Taking out your goods (money / camera etc.).** Before I take out my wallet and/or camera (I have a decent camera) I always check around me. Who is around and where are they? Are they close? Are there other tourists? Are there shopkeepers? Do they seem okay? When I take my money or camera out, I keep my daypack in front of me, that way I can easily slip the purse or camera back in once I'm done. It also keeps any other valuables I may be carrying safe too.

- **Wear your day pack on your front.** Yes, it's dorky, but I do this as a rule in all marketplaces and busy squares where you are rubbing shoulders with everyone around you. It is infinitely safer than keeping it on your back.

- **Get a tourist map.** Having a tourist map makes it easier to see where to go to get help, where the police stations are and important things like toilets.

- **Keep all the key contact numbers on you.** Have the phone number and address of your accommodation (a card is great because you can hand this card over to a taxi driver or police officer or whoever), have the emergency assist number and your travel insurance phone number and policy number on you at all times (these can be saved in your phone or put in a wallet - simple and easy to carry around).

- **Don't go out with expensive stuff at night.** As a general rule, I don't take out my fancy camera at night (unless I know the area and I am going out with a group of friends). Generally, at night I go out with the minimum: cash, directions (including how to get home and how much it's likely to cost - I love my bra for that reason - I always stash enough in there and then some for a taxi ride home), accommodation address & keys, lip gloss and that's about it (depending on where I am, I may also include my phone, tissues and hand gel). I like feeling lighter at night. I am also more relaxed and at ease when I don't have much to lose. So if it does disappear, then no major dramas.

- **Knowing where to and where from.** Knowing where you are coming from and going to is kinda handy for a few reasons, but particularly for safety. Being able to get home is always helpful (if you have a map, you can follow the way the taxi is going as she/he is driving you back).

- **Find out the unsafe areas**. Ask a local and do internet research on which areas to avoid walking around / going to. There will always be a not so good spot in any city and it's easy to avoid it or take extra precautions if you know about the area.

- **Ask a local woman.** Ask a local woman (at your accommodation or cafe etc. - one that is likely to be familiar with the safety concerns of women travelers) about the safety of taxis, other transport and neighborhoods.

- **Find out the words for 'brother' and 'sister' in the local language.** If you address men as 'brother', you are more likely to break down the perceived distance between you and the guy who approaches you. The phrase 'I am your sister' could also be helpful to know. When I traveled to Nepal, everyone calls each other 'brother' and 'sister' (regardless of whether you are related or not). I thought it was beautiful and I wrote a blog post about it. I have now borrowed this idea for the rest of my life, but I think it is particularly useful regarding the theme of safety.

- **Observe other women.** Continuously assess risk wherever you are walking. Generally, populated areas are safer for you personally (although sometimes it can be a haven for pickpockets, depending on the location, so just be more careful of your valuables in this instance). Also see if local women are around. Generally, I feel a lot safer when I see women by themselves or with their families or friends.

Group travel

If you are concerned about safety, why not join a tour group? Tour group travel is immensely popular for all budgets, tastes and ages. You will have a guide who organizes at minimum the travel between places, hotels and some activities. With some types of group travel, everything is organized for you, including all meals.

It depends on what you're after. If you don't want to have to think or negotiate anything, the choice is fully paid for travel. If you're a bit more independent, join a travel group that offers the basics and flexibility to do what you want to do during the day (and/or nights). I have joined basic travel groups before and loved it. I am naturally independent, so I would go and explore by myself most days and join the group for some activities or dinners. As I didn't need to worry about booking accommodation or travel, I was able to relax and enjoy the journey from place to place. I also felt incredibly safe.

The detractions with group travel is that you don't know who you will be traveling with, whether you will have common or no shared interests with the other members of the group. And you are stuck with them for the duration of the trip.

If you're not comfortable with complete self-time yet, it is a good option. It also gets you familiar with the whole travel experience.

Hosteling it

Hostels are a great way to meet other travelers. If you stay at a popular hostel, you are guaranteed to meet people, and usually there are some that you will want to hang out with. If you get in a room of people you don't gel with, ask to swap to another room. It's great practice to introduce yourself as soon as you can so that you can get a feel of who you may want to spend more time with.

My friend Clare who I mentioned above says that making friends is an important part of being safe. I couldn't agree more. She makes friends with others at her hostel, so that if she goes out and doesn't come home that night, someone will notice (who remembers your name and who you are).

Sometimes in risky destinations, she employs a 'buddy system' when she goes out late to clubs and bars. She regularly arrives at her hostel, introduces herself and then finds out who wants to go out that night. Before she goes out, she asks the other woman/women to make sure they watch out for each other and try to go home together. That way, if the group does different things during the evening, someone will try to find you before they go home.

Stay in credible places

Always stay in credible places. What do I mean by this? Stay at places where someone's reputation is on the line. Stay in hostels / hotels where if you leave a bad review, it matters to them. If you rock up to a town and stay at a local hotel that is not connected, there is a far greater safety risk. There are no reputations at stake.

This also applies to accommodation sites like Airbnb or Couchsurfing. Airbnb has a comprehensive review system and the reviews left by hosts and travelers really matter (the review system is blind, where a person can't see the review that was posted about them until they post their review). One bad review and no-one will stay again. With couchsurfing.com it is similar, where hosts can be verified and reviewed. I only stay with hosts that are both verified and positively reviewed.

If it ends up that you have to stay very local, check the physical security of the place. Is there a lock on your door and any outside doors? Are there other tourists staying there? Does it have a family vibe? Assess the risk as soon as you can and try to find other options if it doesn't feel right for you.

Doing stuff not covered by your travel insurance

You will inevitably do things that are not covered by your travel insurance (and most likely you will not even know you are doing it). Thinking about the risks of various activities will most likely not stop you from doing them (well I hope not in most reasonable cases) but at least be aware of the pitfalls of various activities.

For example, riding on a motor bike as a driver or a passenger in Thailand, unless specifically added to your insurance, invalidates your insurance. Yes, it's the cheapest form of transport and a very fun option (if not heart stopping), and you will have to determine whether it's a risk you want to take.

Also, drinking and then having an accident subsequent to consuming alcohol is not usually covered (e.g. breaking an ankle walking home from a drinking session).

Other activities have higher risks, e.g. jumping out of a plane, water ski-ing, jet skis, bungy jumping, all extreme sports or taking illicit substances. You have to weigh up what is going to work for you.

Hitchhiking

I have met some amazing women who have hitchhiked alone through countries I wouldn't dream of not traveling in first class secure vehicles. All power to them, but hey, it's something that I haven't been game enough to do. I was brought up in a time of big 'stranger danger' and infamous backpacker murders close to where I came from and it really made an impression on me.

The women I have met that have hitchhiked by themselves have been able to speak the local language first of all. This really helps a great deal. Firstly, you can assess the driver better. And you can potentially have good conversations!

Secondly, they have dressed down. They have worn loose clothing, not worn make up and have been deliberately 'unladylike' (belching and farting at will).

Thirdly, they have taken a few moments to assess the driver's vehicle before climbing in (do they have pictures of their family? is it warm and inviting or cold and barren?). They've always asked the driver first where they are going and known beforehand the names of the towns along their path towards their destination.

Obviously there are big safety risks, but the women that I've met who have hitchhiked, have gotten to know interesting people and done a lot of traveling for free!

Partying like it's 1999...

There is partying, and then there is partying in one of Rio's infamous favela's until dawn, watching the sunrise over the pretty peaks and curvaceous beaches over one of the world's most beautiful yet dangerous cities. I decided to go to this party because there were a group of people from my hostel that were going who were a perfect mix of fun and sense.

My partying safe recommendations

- **Don't take any illicit substances.** Unless you have a lot of expendable cash and can bribe your way out of going to jail (in countries where bribery is the common rule of law). Also, you don't know what's in that shit - so just don't.

- **Always have an exit plan.** Know how to get home! Stick with your new friends, but leave them if they do anything rash.

- **Don't take anything of value with you.** I carry enough for beer and water and a taxi ride home and that's it.

- **Kissing random strangers.** All cool, as long as your friend has got your back. I always ask my new friends for a second opinion on random people I may or may not kiss. I remember being at a club in Rio and one gentleman showed me, according to him, how people greet people in Brazil. I was never again greeted the same way whilst I was in the country, but it sure was interesting. Apparently, you start by gently kissing someone on each cheek before softly moving to their lips and lingering there for a while…

Planning to go out on the town by yourself

I regularly take myself out to dinner in a new town and then go home. That is super easy. What I've had to do a lot more planning for, is going out on the town by myself late at night.

I regularly stay in accommodation by myself and at these times I don't have a huge opportunity to connect with other travelers (which is completely fine with me, as I enjoy my own company). At these times, there is no-one I can say 'Let's go out on the town tonight!' So what is a girl to do in these situations? Go out by herself of course!

I remember one time in Istanbul. I had fallen in love with the city by day and dusk, the wild ferry rides across the Bosporus, wandering across cobblestones staring up at the impossibly beautiful mosques, being rubbed down by mostly naked women in the heat of 11th century bathhouses, and enjoying the wonder of a warm bowl of corba. I wanted to see if the night life could live up to my daylight infatuations.

To prepare, I got on the web. I found the general clubbing area in Beyoglu and researched places that I thought I would like. Gay bars have always been a good safe option for me (I get hassled less). I was also curious to check out what a gay place would be like in a Muslim country. I thought if I found a few decent looking places, I would have a choice if one turned out to be a non-event.

I saved all the club information, directions on how to get to the club, what was close by so I could find the club I thought I'd check out first. I researched how to get there on public transport and also roughly how much a cab ride home would be. I took photos of the maps of the area and the roads I needed to walk down from the tram stop to the clubbing area.

I took the bare minimum: phone, enough cash (some safely tucked away in my bra), the card from my hotel, lip gloss, tissues and the tram card. I had read that nothing gets going until after 12, but the trams stopped by 11.30pm, so I thought I'd have a wander before heading into the club.

Initially I was a bit worried about a dark walk between the tram stop and the clubs, but I took a gamble on it being busy enough since it was a Saturday night. It turns out it was quite dark and there weren't a lot of people around, so I walked in the middle of the road and just moved to the side when a car went by. As soon as I arrived in the famous Istiklal Avenue however, it was a completely different story.

There was slightly more room to move than during daylight hours. The street was lit up by meshes of noise from shops, bars and people. I had memorized the street map and quickly found the street my club was in (I had a backup photo of the map in my phone as well). I tried as casually as I could to walk down the club street filled with a very diverse range of clubs whilst bouncers and others stared at me. After 2 weeks, I still hadn't gotten used to the amount of male mania I received. I guess my wild blonde hair does little to avoid unwanted attention. I tried to ignore it and look a cross between completely preoccupied and confident. I strutted down the street and spotted the club. It was too early and no-one was around, so I walked back around to the throb of Istiklal Avenue. After wandering about for another 30 mins I tentatively made my way back.

Entering a very sparse club, I made my way to the bar. The music hit me immediately. Such cool sounds! Music like I hadn't heard in any club anywhere, rhythmical, deep voices and hip wanting swagger.

I got a beer, made my way to a sofa and started sipping. I needed something to do, so I took out my phone and starting two finger typing a letter to my best friend. I casually glanced up every now and then and smiled at people moving past. It took another 30 minutes for it to start getting a decent amount of people in.

I loved watching people dance and eventually a group of women approached me and invited me to dance with them. I was a bit nervous, but glad for the offer. They seemed fun and lively. One of them translated for the group. After a few drinks, we were all firm friends. After an hour or so they invited me out for a delicious bowl of corba (no Maccas on the run in Istanbul, warm lentil soup is all the rage), and then onto the next club. More dancing, more drinks, more fun. Eventually I thought I should leave, so two of the group accompanied me to the taxi rank and told the taxi driver where to take me.

I had such a fun night. I learnt more about a different side to Turkish culture, and made new friends. And it was all because I decided to venture out of my comfort zone, *prepared*.

Shit that happens and how to deal with it

The rest of this chapter contains stories from the road and advice on what to do if you get into a not so good feeling situation.

Potential theft

I've been followed a couple of times taking pictures with my large camera. These have been in touristy or populated areas. If I notice, initially I put my camera back into my daypack and walk into the closest cafe. Once a woman followed me into the cafe and sat and waited for me. It was odd. I specifically stared at her to let her know that I knew. I just waited it out and eventually she moved on.

Male advances

More than regularly, I am approached by men (particularly in countries where white women are perceived by men as sexually promiscuous, like the Hollywood movies (because when we see a man of course we automatically fall on our backs and stick our legs in the air), think: India, Turkey, Morocco as examples). Often the men try and get me into conversation. Usually I am polite and make my answers short and say 'nice to meet you' and leave. Sometimes I've had to walk in the opposite direction or go into a cafe to stop them from talking to me. Other times I've gotten a bit annoyed (because they are forceful or over insistent) and said 'I'm not interested'.

Often I'm whistled at or called out at. I ignore these. It seems to be the safest approach to ignore rather than to respond (although on many occasions I would just love to yell 'fuck off' back at them, but I know that could provoke a greater response which I'm not confident I'd be safe in).

When I first started traveling, I was friendlier than I am now. I am still friendly, but it really depends on the person and how they approach me. If they are rude, I have no hesitation of being firm or even rude back. I've had to yell at men sometimes and when I do this, they have backed away.

Also read my two final safety stories for more tips on how I've handled sticky situations to do with men.

Getting ripped off

I hired out a driver for a day out of Ubud, Bali to see some temples and local life in the country. I was warned by my driver that I should not pay any more than a few dollars for a tour of this particular temple. Hordes of guides offered to take me to see the temple. I refused them all and continued to walk up the hill.

One gentleman, following me, told me that my driver had told me the wrong price (I know my driver was correct because I had also read it on some online guides as well). I had just that amount and no more. I explained this to the gentlemen and he said 'Do you have any Australian money?' I said yes, but no change for a $50 note if it was going to cost me 10 or 20 dollars as he suggested.

After some back and forth, I said "I'll just go look myself."

"Come on, I'll show you and I'll even take you back to exchange the money myself and it won't cost you any more than $10." He talked about feeding his family.

I reluctantly followed. He was insistent. But I didn't trust him. I asked him a lot of questions about the temple and he was informative. At the end he said, "That's it."

"Aren't you going to take me back down to exchange the money as promised?"

"No, they don't do that down there."

"But you said."

"I have change."

"Okay."

I was trying to calculate the correct exchange rate as he was handing me back change in Indonesian currency from my $50 Australian note. I was confused, I felt pressured and this man was unrelenting. He handed me back some and I said I needed more. He handed me over more.

"Okay." He went to walk away.

"You said you would drive me back to the entrance."

"You want to be driven back?"

"Yes." *Like it was an option!* He dropped me quickly and sped back up the hill like he wanted to escape something.

My driver's first question to me was, "How much did you pay?"

"Don't ask."

It really put a dampener on my day. I worked out later he swindled me out of at least $25 for a 20-minute tour (plus the offerings he insisted on me paying to the various people as we went around the temple) that should have cost $2.

Although I could see he was only trying to make a living and he was probably feeding a family, the way he went about it, the dishonesty and meanness, to me, was horrendous. This was after a number of incidences in Bali which affected my whole experience of the holiday.

I have often given great tips to my guides when they are have been informative, professional and nice. I like to be generous, but this situation did not allow this.

My recommendations

You are very likely to be swindled out of cash as a solo female traveler. I have had this happen a number of times.

What is interesting in the above story is that I knew about it! I read online about the price; I was warned of the convincing men and even told about it again by my Balinese driver. I even discussed it with the swindler himself of the swindling that occurs. And yet he still ripped me off!

So despite your best efforts, this shit sometimes happens. I take it as part of the traveling experience. I am a lot stronger now in saying 'No' than I used to be and this has happened due to my ongoing travel experiences. I have a more 'Fuck off' sounding 'No' than the polite 'No' I used to have. Believe me, I like being polite and generous, and I really try and take each situation afresh as it comes, but there is a stronger me that emanates now. Yah for her!

Two final safety stories

I want to finish with two stories about personal safety that will give you some tips on how you could handle the situation yourself. These are never fun stories. I share them not to make you scared, but to help you be prepared.

The first is a story of traveling in the wee hours of the morning from Penang in Malaysia to Thailand. It is my most popular blog post ever.

One of those days...

Outside noises woke me at 12.30am and 1.40am. I kept checking my phone, worried I didn't set my alarm, or that it wouldn't go off. I went to bed at midnight.

Crickets chirped on my iPhone waking me at 4am. I blearily headed to the bathroom, splashing myself in an attempt to make something come alive. Anything.

I dressed for a 16-hour day of travel: a roomy comfortable t-shirt and Thai pants (both cool and ever so flexible).

I was downstairs outside my hostel at 4.45am. The colorful 19th century Chinese colonial houses were lit by soft fluoro lights, providing me some light between the pillars. I looked to both ends of the street. Not another animal in sight.

A few motorbikes drove past. I stood at the side of the pavement so that the minivan could see me. I made several calls the day before confirming my early pickup.

5.15am. I make a Skype call. 'Hi, I am waiting for a pick up, it was supposed to be here at 5am. Just making sure the driver knows where to find me?'

'Yes, I have your pick-up. The driver will be there soon.'

Another motorcycle went past. It turned around and drove back down to the end of the street. It turned around again and drove back down to the other end of the street. Again the motorcycle passed. It turned around for the fourth time.

On the fifth time, it slowed down almost pulling to a stop about two meters away from me. My stomach started knotting. Feelings of both anger and unease washed over me.

"Fuck off!"

The solidly built man stared at me.

"Just fuck off."

His bike roared into action. He turned around pulling up the bike so that he was just a meter from me.

"What did you say to me? Your stupid mouth. Shut up your stupid mouth."

I stood there looking at him. I involuntarily took a step backwards. I looked around me. There weren't any escape routes. I couldn't get back into the hostel; I had locked myself out as requested. I could run either right or left with my heavy backpack.

"Your stupid mouth, you think you're that beautiful. Have you looked at yourself in the mirror lately? Your stupid mouth."

"Fuck off."

"You wanna fuck? Your stupid mouth needs this cock." He grabs himself. "You stupid woman. You stupid whore."

He continued to hurl such pleasantries at me for another few minutes. I knew it was pointless to respond. Pointless to run.

I stood motionless. *Please make him go!*

In a pause I repeated. "Just fuck off."

He stared at me again. I stared back.

He started up his bike. And drove slowly down the street.

I started to become more anxious. He could come back. With friends. *Is the minivan ever going to get here?*

I looked at my phone. 5.25am.

"Hello, I am still waiting for my pick up."

"What's the address again?"

I sigh and explain the roads the hostel runs off. "Ok, ok, driver will be there."

Another bike drives past. The driver looks at me and slows down pulling to a stop on the other side of the narrow road.

He waves with a big smile, "Hello baby!"

"Go away."

"Ok, ok." He drives off.

I breathe out. His energy was different than the first. Friendlier, but my emotions were marching up and down my blood stream on high alert. *I hope the first doesn't come back. Or bring his friends. Shit, I hope the minivan comes soon.*

I begin to move back behind a pillar, trying to make myself less obvious to the random bike driving past.

5.40am.

"Hello. I am still waiting for the driver."

"Can you get a taxi?"

"There are no taxis in sight. I would come to you, but the streets are dark and there's no-one around."

"He'll be there. Where is it again?"

I patiently explain the address again.

"Will I need to call back? Are you sure he's coming? I'm getting harassed on the street. I really need to know he's coming."

"He'll be there. No need to call back."

I started to get the overwhelming need to go to the toilet.

Desperately. The kind of desperation a person gets after eating something from a grimy food stall in Asia. I needlessly looked around the street again. I couldn't miss the minivan. I couldn't get back into my hostel.

Could I go on the street? What if a motorbike came past and caught me? How much worse would that be? And what about the poor pedestrians later in the morning?

I banged on the door of the hostel in the vain hope someone might hear me and get up. Nothing.

I tried deep breathing. I tried to focus on something else.

5.55am

A female voice answers.

"Hi, I had a 5am pick up. I'm at … Is the driver coming? »

"Where are you?"

I explain the address again and the streets it borders adding "I'm not very far from your office."

"Ok, I'll let the driver know."

"I've already called three times this morning and twice yesterday. I need to get this minivan; I have to get to Thailand this morning."

"Ok, I'll get the driver to pick you up."

6.13am

Same female voice. "The driver couldn't find you, he's gone to Thailand. You'll have to wait for another bus midday today."

"I can't wait. I have to get to Thailand this morning, my travel is coordinated so I can get the last ferry."

"There is nothing I can do."

"What? This is my fifth call this morning, I called yesterday. I have been harassed by men on the street. I am desperately in need of a toilet, and I can't get back into my hostel."

Two young loud men walk past me on the street, "Hey girl? What do you want to do?' Waving their arms in an unsavory manner at me."

"Look, I'm getting harassed again. This is too much. It's unsafe. I need to get to Thailand."

"The driver can't find you. He's Thai, he's not from here."

"That's his job! That's not good enough. You need to show him. I have been calling all morning. I have been waiting alone in the dark and been harassed on the street. Do you know what that's like? I have to get the last ferry"

Silence.

She's hung up on me!

I bang on the door to the hostel again. I'm beyond emotional. The closest I can get to describing myself at that moment is a fish on dry land trying shit and breathe at the same time.

I start pacing. The dawn was on its way and I saw more movement of cars down one end of the street.

After about 5 minutes, I reluctantly make myself call back.

'Hi, its me."

"I have asked the driver to turn around. He's coming back. Where can you go that he find you."

"Umm I know this hotel a few streets away, do you know…"

"No."

"Look I can walk into your office in about 15 minutes. Its lighter now and there's more people, so I think it'll be ok."

"Do you know where we are? Maybe you could meet him at a bank."

"No, I know where you are. I've been there before. At least we'll both know where it is." *Side note, I had been there once, at 9pm at night, two nights before after a 16 hour travel day, but I was sure I would find it again.*

'Have you got a number so I can call you?"

"No, I don't. I'm calling through Wi-Fi."

"Take my number then."

I walk briskly down the end of the street. I notice a restaurant off the main road. I ask the first person I see for a toilet. Relief is the wrong word. More like that fish getting another chance of life-water kinda feeling.

I'm almost there. I walk around the huge building trying to recognize all the entrances and exits. Eventually I found the right looking one.

I walk up to a woman looking up and down the under-building street.

"*It's you?* Quickly, quickly."

And with that, I'm scrambled into the minivan.

I wish I could say that was the end of the delirium that continued to unfold throughout the day. I was over and above exhaustion. Missing transport connections and being put on others. I witnessed corruption (many times). I lent a stranger a lot of money, not knowing if I'd see it again. I did. I had to fight again to be fairly treated. I lost.

I made the last ferry by two minutes.

I was crying by the time I made it back to my bungalow. I cried myself to sleep. I was safe, but alone and feeble.

The only solution the next day was to eat pancakes and chocolate. And organize Skype chats to debrief with friends. It took more than a few days to get back to feeling somewhat normal. I felt numb and overwhelmed. I cried some more.

Of course there were a range of factors in this event that played its part. Not the least of which was that I was also menstruating.

This is one of the worst kinds of days you experience as a solo female traveler. No-one to share the burden. No-one to help negotiate. No-one to stick up for you. No shoulder to cry on. No-one to debrief to. No one to be kind to you.

Except you.

And I survived. But it took its emotional toll. It ran me dry. More than depleting. So I took care of myself in the following days, reading, eating and talking to close friends (thank you!). I am fortunate enough to have been able to do this. Some others aren't.

I wanted to share this day because of the unique experiences of being a woman traveling by herself. I know much of what I experienced as a woman I would not have experienced if I was a man (sexual harassment, being treated differently on pick up, not having to fight to be taken seriously, feeling more personally comfortable to walk in dark streets, and the list goes on. I won't list all the research on all this, needless to say, it's universal).

But this day (and those I've had before), does not make me want to stop traveling. These days are extreme. And the good days, the magnificent sights, learnings, sharings, wonder and pure joy strongly outweigh these types of days for me.

But sometimes, just sometimes, I wish for a traveling companion.

...

The second and final story I want to share with you is my journey from Varanasi to Delhi in India.

Varanasi to Delhi

"Do you have any updated information on the train to Delhi and a platform number?"

"Yes, Platform 6. 30 minutes." I looked at him. *We both know that that is a definitely 'maybe 30 minutes' and it is possibly platform 4 or 6.*

Plodding slowly up the platform stairs to the overhead walkway, I am overtaken by swarms of spindly people. Making my way just as cautiously down to the platform, I try to avoid the piles of dung, crouching bodies, and a cow. I look around to try and work out how on earth the cow got on this platform. She is in the middle of at least 8 platforms and the only way to get to each platform is via the stairs, and as far as I know, cows can't climb stairs. The only reasonable explanation I can come up with is that in India, miraculous flying cows demonstrate their sacredness and god status by choosing to hang out at Platform 6.

Carefully maneuvering my way around the cow, piles of plastic, multicolored dirt, humans squatting, staring & eating, I search for a place to put my backpack down. It was a fruitless thought. I simply could not bear the thought of my backpack touching the ground here.

Resolving to lean my backpack and myself against a wall for a while, I wait. An hour or so passes with me eventually finding the least dirty spot for me to place my backpack down. I see a train coming in and I rush to jump-dance my backpack on. I have no idea how long the train will be stopping.

Looking for my carriage and still unsure whether it was the correct train, a man approaches me.

"Ticket... no, your carriage far away, quickly, train not stop long."

I try jogging with my 30 kilos and continue to hand over my ticket to random men who continue to ask for it, who continue to point further and further down the train. Eventually a man tells me to get into a carriage. I clamber up the steep stairs, desperately trying to follow the one who has kept my ticket.

He opens the door to a cabin. There are four men sitting on two beds. I can't see any other beds. *This is supposed to be first class!*

"This is your cabin. And your bed is up here." He motions for a man to get off the bed below and he pulls a top bed down from the wall.

"I will get you sheets."

The four middle aged men are staring at me as I scramble to put up my front 12 kilo pack on the top bed. I push my large backpack under one of the bottom beds. I feel eight eyes all over me. My heart rate quickens. The men are now completely silent. When the ticket man opened the door they all seemed to be in great conversation with one another. Not now.

I scramble onto the top bunk to sort myself out when the ticket guy comes back with the sheets. *I don't want to even touch this bed.* The bed displays old patches of joy that has been. *Delightful.* Oh why did I not fly to Delhi? Because the first class train was an eighth of the cost. *That's why.*

There is continued silence as I flounder around with my sheets. I sneak looks towards the men only to catch them fixated on me. My heart skips a few beats. I can't get off now and I have to get to Delhi to catch my connecting flight.

The reality begins to set in: I am stuck in this wardrobe of a room with these men for over 16 hours. *Fuck.*

It is clearly not safe.

I race through my head for options, and come up with none that could help me. I didn't see any women in the other carriages I passed. And the train is clearly all booked up. So I resolve to do the only thing I could.

I climbed down to the bottom and tentatively sat on the bed opposite to where 4 men were sitting. The whole space between the two ground beds was barely hip width. This did nothing to diminish the tension.

"Namaste." I tried to look each man in the eye.

A couple averted their eyes from me, looking down and two mumbled "Namaste."

"My name is Sunni. What's yours?" I tried to keep it upbeat.

Some pretended that they didn't speak English. If they are in first class, it is almost certain they know how to speak English.

One man told me his name and then the others.

"Nice to meet you. I'm from Australia."

"Australia…" more mumbling ensued.

"Where are you going to?"

"I'm going to Delhi, then Dharmsala."

"Dharmsala." They nod.

It got uncomfortably silent again.

"Ok, I'm going to rest. Nice to meet you."

I pulled myself back up onto my bed. My heart was still letting me know she wasn't comfortable.

What the f' am I going to do? I decide to put a pen and my pocket knife under my pillow. Moving them to my pillow as subtly as I could, I felt eight eyes continuing to bare into me.

I get out a book and pretend to read. I try and focus on the pages. I'm exhausted but I know it'll be impossible to sleep.

"Chaaoooooiiiiii, Chaaaaiiiiiiii, Chaaarrriiiiiiii"

The door opens, I nod and hold up a finger.

Clasping the small hot cup and I hand over 10 Rupees. I look around to catch the mens' attention.

"I love Chai."

Some nod. Some smile. I resolve to order Chai each time someone comes around. I don't care if it makes me want to use what they call a toilet in the train which essentially resembles a hole in the ground of a muddy winter's yard. It makes me more like them.

As the afternoon stretches out, I order a vegetarian meal, and continue drinking every Chai that passes. I hold it each time as long as I can before bracing myself for the onslaught of the stench hole around the corner from our cabin.

I notice that they seem to be getting used to me. One even pays for a Chai for me when I don't have any small change left.

But I still don't feel at ease. Far from it.

The men continue to talk in what I presume is Hindi. I can't decide whether it was good I didn't understand what they were discussing or not.

I turned to face the wall and close my eyes. It's all I can do when darkness descends. *How am I going to prepare myself if the inevitable happens?* I feel under my pillow for the hard instruments.

I must have dozed off when there is a loud knock at the door. I notice that the men have locked us into the cabin. *What? They can lock us in from the inside??? Fuck.*

The door opens, a new man enters. I notice a vacant bed he takes up. *It must have been the door noises I heard earlier when one of them left.*

I try not to think about a new man in the dynamic of the room. *He doesn't yet know me. This makes it infinitely more dangerous.* I hear the click of the lock again. *Why do they have to lock it? So that others don't come in.* I'm not sure what's worse.

Wide awake, I continue to stare at the wall. I try not to move. *Less movement the better. Maybe it'll be like I'm dead. They won't want to touch me then.*

It's dark and I can't get the thoughts to stop flooding my mind. I've seen how women are treated in India. Rapes and sexual assaults are extremely common. Every moment I've walked out of my hotel in India, I've been continuously stared at, harassed, followed and hounded. Being on constant alert, wary and overly firm with my interactions with men here has been more than exhausting.

Eventually, and what seemed like an eternity, I heard the call that we were approaching Delhi. Light was just beginning to herald on the horizon. *Wow, I think I've made it.*

As I exited the train, I noticed swarms of men and not a woman in sight. Later on I found out that woman in India as a rule, don't travel by themselves, (except by necessity), and only travel with their families.

I decide then and there never to catch an overnight train by myself in India ever, ever, again. I love India and I definitely want to travel there in the future to explore more of this amazing country. However, I won't travel in a train or bus overnight by myself. And I highly recommend if you are considering traveling to India to join a group tour. It's a place like no other, and you should visit, but be safe. Go on a tour!

The Ultimate Safety List

- ✔ Avoid arriving at night to a new place. Arriving during daylight hours is not only safer, you can also gauge a better feel of a town generally and also around your accommodation.

- ✔ Go and explore prepared! Know where you are going and how to get there.

- ✔ Know your limits!

- ✔ Don't go out with expensive stuff at night.

- ✔ Have an entry and exit plan when you go out at night.

- ✔ Treat and speak to everyone like they are your brother and sister. Say the words 'brother' and 'sister' to people in their language if possible. It is a way to instantly create a connection between you and them.

- ✔ Look people in the eye and talk to them directly. Appear confident, even when your insides are a bowl of mushy peas.

- ✔ Be insistent. Don't take 'no' for an answer when you are alone (or anytime really).

- ✔ It's okay to say 'Fuck off' when someone is annoying you. If they don't understand or take it the wrong way, it's their problem. Not yours.

- ✔ Know what's in your travel insurance (and what's not covered).

✔ Never leave your accommodation without your accommodation address and phone number.

✔ Always carry the country's emergency numbers.

✔ Always have your phone fully charged before you leave to your next destination! Turn it off whilst you are sleeping on your mode of transport (if it's safe). And turn it off if you get to a quarter use or so before your destination. It's better to have silence on some of your journey (i.e. no music) rather than not be able to find your accommodation when you arrive.

✔ I regularly take photographs of maps where I need to go, so I have a record of it to follow. No Wi-Fi needed! I think it's good practice anyway because you never know whether you'll be connected or the connection drops somewhere.

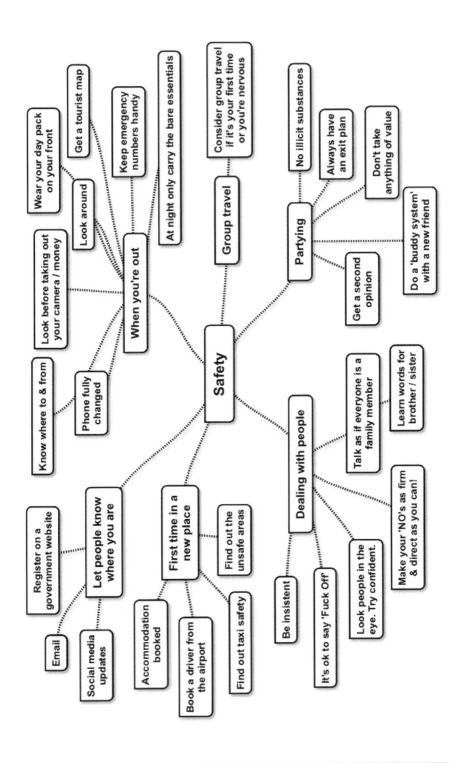

Safety

When you're out
- Wear your day pack on your front
- Get a tourist map
- Keep emergency numbers handy
- Look around
- At night only carry the bare essentials
- Look before taking out your camera / money
- Know where to & from
- Phone fully changed

Group travel
- Consider group travel if it's your first time or you're nervous

Partying
- No illicit substances
- Always have an exit plan
- Don't take anything of value
- Do a 'buddy system' with a new friend
- Get a second opinion

Let people know where you are
- Register on a government website
- Email
- Social media updates

First time in a new place
- Find out the unsafe areas
- Accommodation booked
- Book a driver from the airport
- Find out taxi safety

Dealing with people
- Talk as if everyone is a family member
- Learn words for brother / sister
- Be insistent
- It's ok to say 'Fuck Off'
- Look people in the eye. Try confident.
- Make your 'NO's as firm & direct as you can!

11. Traveling home

The home journey. Dreaded by most. Loved by some. Most people look forward to familiar things going home: your bed, companion animals, friends, family, loved ones and your local. The first meetings are usually fun and lively loved-up interactions.

The truth is, it doesn't last long. There is the usual excitement when you get back, but quickly things return to the status quo. This happens in all your circles: work, friend, hobby, sport etc.

No-one really cares but you

Your friends haven't experienced anything you have. Some may want a few more details, but most aren't interested in talking about the intricate details of your travels (highlights are usually more than enough). Your peeps are naturally interested most in what's happening for them. And that's cool. But it may leave you feeling just a little blue.

What you can do about it

Keep your travels alive. You can do this in many ways:

- Sort through your photos.

- Upload your photos to your social media pages.

- Print some pics out and put them on your wall or fridge or back of the toilet door.

- Connect again with friends from the road.

- Talk with a friend who's traveled a lot - go for drinks and discuss travel tales.

- Think about what you really want to be spending your time on (it's great time to reflect on your work/life path and whether it's working for you - talk to a coach if you need some help with this). Importantly, make a plan and work towards it every week. It will make you feel better, I promise.

- Talk to someone who cares (like a coach or a friend who has traveled and loved it and has had the travel slump before). One colleague randomly asked me weeks and months after coming back - what was your favorite meal... what did Oaxaca smell like? (she was lovingly reminding me to remember my travels and I loved her for that). Find a buddy you can do that with.

- And there's always the tried and true: plan your next adventure!

Going Home Checklist

- ✔ Got your presents? (or is your sparkling presence enough?
- ✔ Got remembering gifts for you?
- ✔ Arranged a pick up or love up at the airport?
- ✔ Got your keys accessible? Local money ready?
- ✔ Passport?
- ✔ Travel music (something that makes you happy or makes you remember a moment from your travels - if you've been anywhere near a beach Bob Marley will be a sound choice).

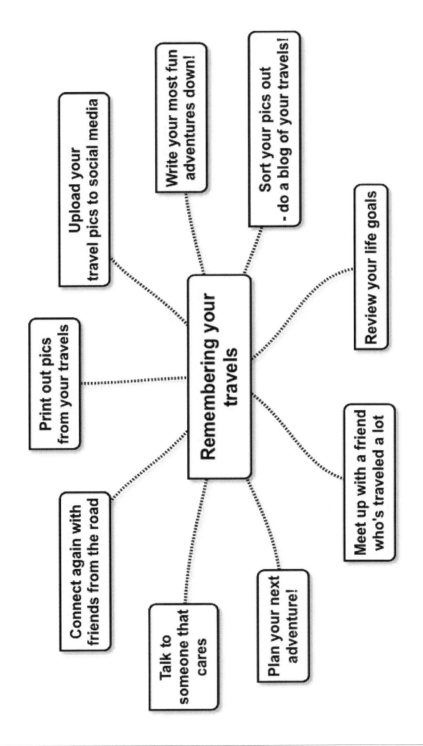

Remembering your travels

- Upload your travel pics to social media
- Write your most fun adventures down!
- Sort your pics out - do a blog of your travels!
- Review your life goals
- Print out pics from your travels
- Meet up with a friend who's traveled a lot
- Connect again with friends from the road
- Talk to someone that cares
- Plan your next adventure!

12. Traveling cheaply & living abroad

So you're on a budget?

There are so many ways to travel on the cheap. Traveling of course is very different to living abroad, but there are some useful tips and insight you can gain in knowing about both (and this may potentially inspire you to spend some lengthier times abroad!). Many of the ideas below you can do for shorter or longer periods of time. It is completely up to you.

Ideas for traveling on the cheap

Stop longer and move less

Stay in a place for a longer period of time. Traveling from place to place every couple of days is not only costly, it is also tiring. This is something worth thinking about.

Many people want to travel to as many places as they can, ticking off their ever increasing bucket list. A few questions for you to consider: what are your aims for your holiday? Do you want to come home exhausted or refreshed?; do you want to stop and smell the flowers?; do you want to go 24/7 and fit in as much as you can?

I personally have found that staying a bit longer in a place enables me to get to know a place better and the people better. I find a local restaurant and cafe that becomes my haunt. The waiters recognize me, become friendlier and I get to have more and better conversations with those around. I'm also not so tired. I get to see more things in the one city. I get to feel her better.

I might not see the 10 places in the country that you 'must see', (and if you don't, you'll be as significant as a dot on a Dalmatian), but instead I get a deeper understanding of a culture and town.

These days, if possible, I stay for months in one spot. Staying for a longer period of time, I get to go to my local hangouts, get known by my favorite local cafes and languish in the every day.

Then I create a new every day in the next country and town.

Of course it all depends on how long you have to travel, your budget and your contentedness level. Can you be content in one place for longer? Do you have the itch to move every few days? Do you like to relax or run around like a head waiter at the Ritz?

Stay or travel in a cheap country / place

The cost of traveling for a month in South East Asia is vastly different from spending a month in Scandinavia, for example. You will get very different traveling experiences in either location. If you are on a budget, Asia is an obvious choice. Certainly you can travel more cheaply in Scandinavia if you don't eat out, catch local transport, couchsurf or volunteer (see below for further ideas), but in South East Asia you could have your own bungalow in a forest or beach, drink Mai Tais and have a massage every second day for the same amount as your basic incidental daily cost in Scandinavia.

Again it depends on the type of experience you are after. To do Scandinavia for the same cost as South East Asia will mean you will have to share homes (and find free places to stay), and eat supermarket food. This may be great if you want to make local friends and learn about Scandinavian culture. If you are after more self-reflection time, a cheap bungalow on a Thai island can cost you the same and give you the space you need.

Use local transport

There are usually multiple ways you can get from place to place. Obviously traveling using local transport is the cheapest (although usually not the easiest, depending on your location). See Chapter 'Traveling once you're there' for tips on how to do this.

Ideas for living on the cheap

Most people are curious about how I've managed to travel and live overseas for many years. I've had a number of fortuitous circumstances, but the fundamental truth is that I have not been concerned with following a standard career and life path. If I was, I would be currently living back in my home town with a great job and career prospects, a partner, house and perhaps some kids.

Instead I've chosen a life where I am not sure where I'm going to be living in a month's time (or two. These days I'm very comfortable with this, although there was a time in the not so distant past when I would have been petrified at this thought). I am single and I have no desire to bear children (I'm satisfied in caring for other people's children, adults and non human animals that cross my path). I live very cheaply, spending money only on food and essential living expenses. I am happy with a backpack full of my necessities. I don't need anything else.

I am also satisfied with how I'm contributing to the world through my writing, volunteering, developing my books and blogs (including helping people embrace change and live more bravely), connections I make on the road and my friends I keep in touch with from across the globe.

I understand this is not a life for everyone. I also understand that life can change and morph at different times. Maybe you want to have wonderful holidays and get back into your home life. Great! Maybe you want to have a 6 month break to explore the world and/or you for a while. Wonderful! Maybe you want to push yourself to new heights, do something you didn't think you were capable of. Awesome!

These are all marvelous options. You might try something and realize it's not for you. That's totally cool too. Allow yourself to play with different options and ideas. There is no right or wrong in this, try something and if it doesn't work, try something else. It is all good. The rest of this chapter are some of the ways I've lived on the cheap. It's a start for your travel / life preparations.

Live in a cheap country

You may have read the random articles that circulate every six months or so ('Top cheap locales to live for a year'). It is true there are many places on this earth that you can live cheaply for long periods of time, and this can change dramatically depending on economic and political happenings in the country. Living abroad requires quite some research.

What you need to research

- **Visas.** Visa requirements vary throughout the world depending on where you are from and where you are going to. Some countries update and change their visa requirements regularly, so check with the country's embassy before you go. You may need to exit and re-enter the country during your stay to continue the currency of the visa.

- **Types of accommodation.** Prices and accommodation differ greatly in any city. You can research online before you leave. You may want to book the first few nights or first week's accommodation in advance and find out about potential cheaper options for longer term stays after you arrive (often when people meet you face to face and see that you genuinely want to stay for a decent period of time, they are more likely to do a deal with you).

- **The location.** Inevitably there will be more expensive locations to stay in any town. I've found that you can only do so much investigation online. Often when you arrive, you can get a better understanding and 'feel' of a place and where you would prefer to be based.

- **Transport.** Is it easy to get around using public transport? Would you need to hire a vehicle? Can you walk to the shops?

- **Do you need to speak a fair amount of the language?** Some cheaper locales may mean there are not as many tourists, therefore English may not be widely spoken. Do you need to learn the language? How difficult will this be for you?

- **Can you get access to things that you need to enjoy life there?** e.g. How good is the Wi-Fi? If you have eating requirements, can you get the products you need to survive happily?

Some ways to research a bit more about a place you'd like to live in is to join a FB group for ex-pats living in that location (I've found that usually there are a few FB groups for any major city or popular ex-pat destinations). I've often found everything I need to know through these groups from people who have lived there or are currently living there.

You can also get information by posting on a local internations.org or couchsurfing.com forum for the city you want to live in.

Pet and housesitting

I love pet and house sitting. Initially I house sat and looked after my friends' companion animals. Then I researched and signed up for a few house sitting sites in Australia, where I'm from. At the same time, I found an international house and pet sitting website that I decided to create a profile with.

It is this international pet sitting website that I have used to pet and house sit both in Australia and now around the world.

There are professional house and pet sitters that charge for their services. Although I think the competition with those willing to do it for free is on the rise with respected international house sitting websites being trusted more every day.

As a companion animal and house sitter, I do not charge for minding a home or pets, but in return I get a comfortable place to stay, (including all the things I need to live comfortably: Wi-Fi, heating/cooling etc.), non human animal company and an opportunity to explore a whole new world!) Not paying for accommodation and associated bills means there is a huge chunk more to use for either enjoying the town you stay or continuing your travels afterwards.

What you need to be a house/pet sitter: a great communicator (be responsive to emails back and forth); you must love non human animals and be attentive to their needs (and be able to clearly demonstrate this); flexible (and follow the same routines - some owners want me to have their companion animals sleep with me in my bed) and practical (quickly respond to and solve any issues that arise).

Volunteering

Volunteering is a great way to get to know a place, country and peoples. There are simply so many volunteering opportunities out there catering to both skilled and unskilled workers. I think the primary thing you need to have as a volunteer is willingness. Willingness to learn, work, participate and grow.

I have found the best way to be a volunteer is to be open and curious. I love to learn from everyone I'm with. If I can't speak the language, I learn enough words to be able to communicate the basics. It is always fun to learn language from locals. Especially when you get it wrong. Sometimes very wrong. But it is always thoroughly amusing for those involved. And that is a very good thing in relationship development!

I have volunteered in both skilled and non-skilled capacities. When I volunteer using my professional skills, it can sometimes be very much like work back home (but living and learning another culture is, in itself, very different). I love doing unskilled work. Unskilled work can be incredibly rewarding because often you see the results of your work quicker than typing on a computer all day. You can see painted furniture, a clean room, a built wall, completed house etc.

Work your way around the world

There are many ways you can live for free and work your way around the world. Some people use the term 'volunteering', however, the traditional meaning of volunteering is that you don't receive anything in return for your work or time. There are many websites that enable people to work in exchange for food and accommodation, anywhere in the world.

It is a great idea for small family run businesses, farms, small NGOs, charities and other small businesses that cannot afford to pay traditional wages, but are able to provide accommodation and food and enjoy hosting people. The most common exchange is that you work 4 to 5 hours a day about 5 days each week in exchange for accommodation and food (usually about 2 meals are provided each day).

I have met many people that have worked their way around the world in a variety of capacities and learnt a lot about a place, made lasting friendships and had fantastic experiences. Check out these websites for some inspiration:

www.helpx.net

www.workaway.info

www.betterplace.org

www.ecoteer.com

www.the7interchange.com

www.volunteersbase.com

Hostels

Often hostels offer travelers an opportunity to work at the hostel for a certain number of hours a day (for 5 or 6 days a week) in exchange for free accommodation. You have to love people, hostels and other travelers. And of course be good with providing information and directions (which is a great way to see a city in itself).

Wwoofing

Wwoofing stands for willing workers on organic farms or worldwide opportunities on organic farms. You volunteer your time for food, accommodation and knowledge about organic farming (usually about 4 - 6 hours a day). I know many people who have worked on organic farms across the world. One couple I know wwoof'd throughout Italy for 9 months with their 2-year-old. Awesome.

Becoming crew on a boat

Many people travel the world by working on boats. Or sharing with someone who wants help with running their boat to a particular location. Of course you have to like water and boats and living at sea for long periods of time. You can join a boat as professional staff (trained sailor or captain) or as an amateur.

Check out these sites to start your search:

www.crewbay.com

www.workonboats.com

www.crewseekers.net

www.sailnet.com

Teach English

One of the first things you will need to do to teach English is get a TEFL or TESOL certificate. There are numerous companies online and also courses in thousands of cities worldwide that offer this qualification.

Secondly, you need to decide and assess the merits of a particular country you may want to teach in. Some countries are more affluent and are likely to give decent wages (enabling you to save money for future endeavors/travels), others not so much, but maybe you are attracted to the country for different reasons and perhaps you want to learn the local language or see the particular location.

Thirdly, do close research on the company you are thinking of working for. Go on international teach English forums and check out reviews. I've heard some horror stories of long hours and no payment. There are also excellent places where the work is rewarding and you get fantastic benefits.

Study abroad

There are ample opportunities to study abroad. Some are expensive options, whilst a few countries in Europe offer free study or study at a reduced cost. You could study a language or pursue your field of interest. Sometimes scholarships are offered and usually you are able to work for a certain amount of hours under your study visa.

Living abroad for long periods of time

I travel consistently for years on end. Although these days, I don't actually see myself as traveling. Rather, I consider myself as living in the world and each country I live in for a time is my home. I don't move about any particular country as much as I did previously. I usually move to a spot and set up for a month or three.

This really enables me to feel at home, make new friends and focus on my writing. I get to understand a place, peoples and cultures more whilst I'm there. I really enjoy this.

I use all of the techniques I've mentioned throughout this book in each location I visit. For example, to make friends I use meetup.com or internations.org or couchsurfing.com. These are all great ways to meet likeminded people and I usually find a few people I'd like to hang out with more. If you are volunteering at a particular location or working in the ways I've mentioned above, you will meet people straight away, so in terms of making friends it is even easier.

There are of course drawbacks. Making friends in a particular location, and getting to know them well means that it is often hard to say 'goodbye'. In dealing with this, I use all of the techniques I've outlined in Chapter 'Debriefing and looking after you'.

Another issue that I've encountered is that it's harder to maintain relationships with friends back home. I use social media, but some of my friends aren't as active as me. It's regularly hard to find a time to Skype with friends (especially on different time zones) when everyone is busy with their lives (work, children, routines etc.). At times it can feel very isolating, especially as you are solo and can be half a world away, literally.

I've found that I need to be the one to initiate contact with my friends back home. Because I'm not present, it's hard for people to feel as connected, so I randomly send a personal email, make a phone call (especially birthdays) and also see if they want to Skype.

When I go back home, I have found the friendships are usually still the same (warm and familiar), and there has just been a time gap. As I mentioned in the chapter 'Going home', my friends have had very full lives back home, which are very different to my life experiences. So there is a limit to extensive travel conversations. Of course my friends are naturally focused on what's consumed their lives and I enjoy hearing what they've been through.

What has helped me when I do go back home is to talk with my friends who have had long stints abroad and also connect again with my friends that I met whilst traveling. I also do all the things I love about home. I pretend I'm a tourist in my own city. This can be a fun way to re-introduce yourself to familiar and new haunts (and there are always new places that have sprung up if you've been gone for any length of time).

Getting back into a regular routine and work can also be a challenge. I take the time to refocus my future goals during this time (hence avoiding languishing too much in my exotic past) so that I'm working towards something that I now want. This helps the travel slump immensely. I also try new things outside of work and meet new people. This helps because many of my friends have had children and are not as able to freely go out as they did before.

Travel makes you 'get out there' more and become more confident. I've found that I am a lot more confident even back home now than I ever was before. I feel more sure of myself in making new connections, rekindling older connections and focusing on what I want (which is continuously evolving). I believe solo travel can do that for you too.

I really believe that the fears, potential safety risks, down times and isolated times are tiny compared to the learning opportunities, the new sights and scents, the awe at experiencing something new for the first time, the sunsets, cocktails, joy at making beautiful new connections and all the other richness solo travel has to offer. It is all a part of the journey.

I would love to hear about your stories when you do make the leap. Come join the 'Live Brave' community on FB (https://web.facebook.com/groups/livebrave/).

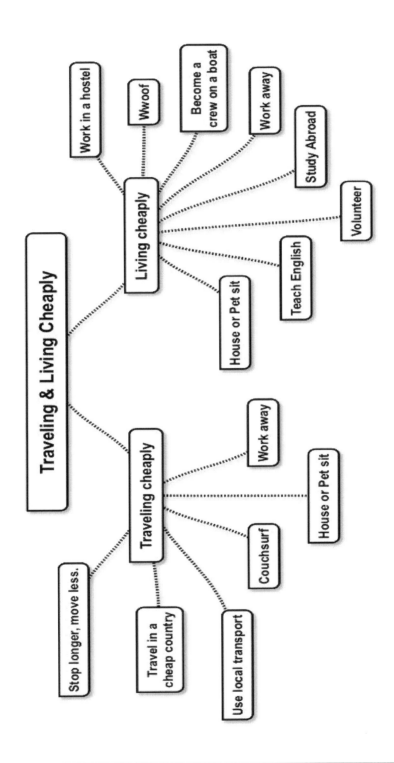

Stay tuned…

My book 'the Secret Diaries of a Solo Woman Traveler' is due out in July 2016. It's saucy, fun and a real adventure between many countries, places and sheets. Be the first to find out it's release. Sign up to my email list on sunnidawson.com.

Dedication

This book is dedicated to you and all the gutsy things you do. You rock. In every way. Live Brave. Inspire you.

This book is also dedicated to women with differing abilities.

Traveling with a disability is a whole other ball game. This book is written from the privileged vantage point of a person that does not need to consider any disability whilst traveling. Obviously, a lot more planning would be required for people with differing abilities. But this book will give you the first 10 steps into your journey of solo travel... and then, if you're keen, you can write the next 10 for solo travel for women with differing abilities!

Thank you...

I'd like thank you for reading. If you enjoyed this book, I'd appreciate it if you left a review. If you didn't, I am very open for any feedback you may have. Thank you! Connect with me through my website: sunnidawson.com and/or my social media pages.

I'd really like to thank Kim Hemingway for being the most amazingly entertaining and awesome friend (and for her great proofreading) and Clare White for her tips and insightful advice. I'd also like to thank Pamela Anderson, Freelance Editor, for her final proofreading (www.fiverr.com/pamelaanderson6). Finally, I want to thank Nadia Rahim and her amazing family for all their support and love.

About the Author

Sunni Dawson is a writer, coach and speaker. She has traveled and lived all over the world for the best part of 5 years. She is passionate about living brave, helping people step outside their comfort zones, curious about what makes people change and loves connecting with people from around the globe. She adores solo travel, cooking and photography. Some of her previous work incarnations include: lawyer, strategic and business planner, call centre chick, diversity specialist, law lecturer and a vego cook for a child care centre.

Check out Sunni's work:

www.sunnidawson.com

YouTube: Sunni Dawson

Facebook: www.facebook.com/sunnidawson

Twitter: www.twitter.com/sunnidawson

Instagram: @sunnidawson

Join the Live Brave FB Community! People who are living brave, making changes, taking risks and supporting each other along the way. Come and be a part of it.

https://web.facebook.com/groups/livebrave/

or email us: livebrave@groups.facebook.com

Notes

Notes

Notes

Made in the USA
Middletown, DE
20 March 2017